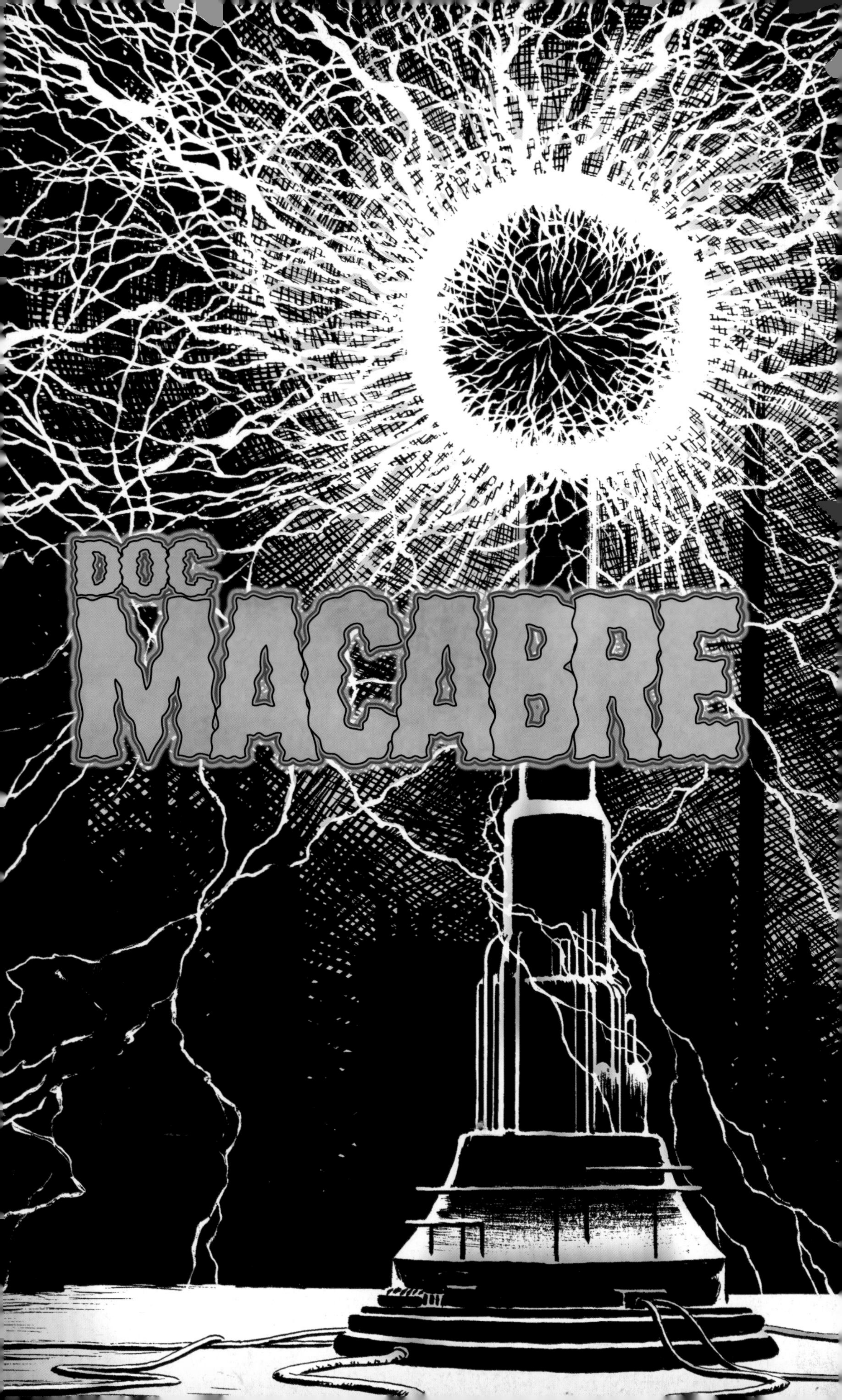
DOC
MACABRE

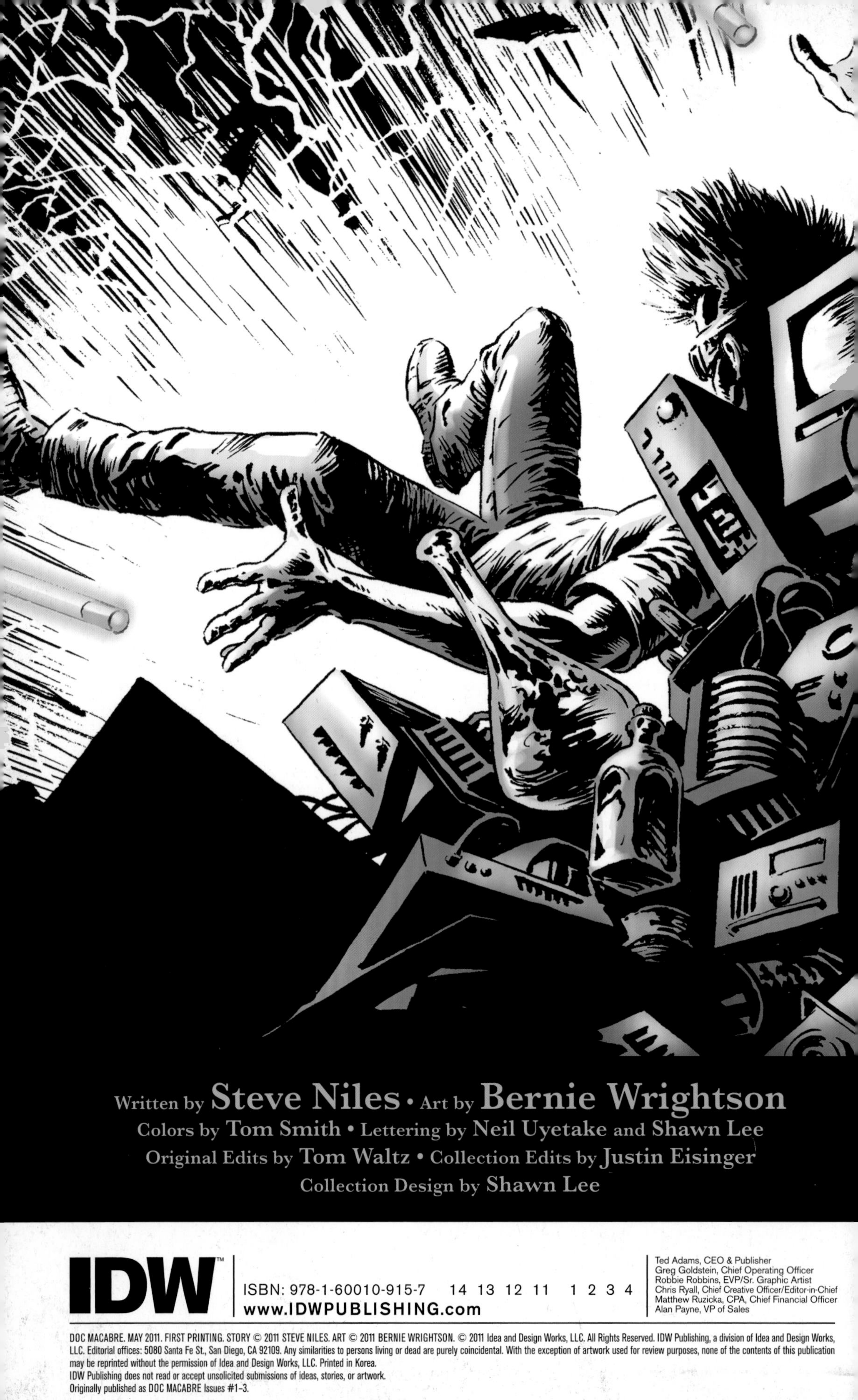

Written by Steve Niles • Art by Bernie Wrightson
Colors by Tom Smith • Lettering by Neil Uyetake and Shawn Lee
Original Edits by Tom Waltz • Collection Edits by Justin Eisinger
Collection Design by Shawn Lee

IDW™

ISBN: 978-1-60010-915-7   14 13 12 11   1 2 3 4
www.IDWPUBLISHING.com

Ted Adams, CEO & Publisher
Greg Goldstein, Chief Operating Officer
Robbie Robbins, EVP/Sr. Graphic Artist
Chris Ryall, Chief Creative Officer/Editor-in-Chief
Matthew Ruzicka, CPA, Chief Financial Officer
Alan Payne, VP of Sales

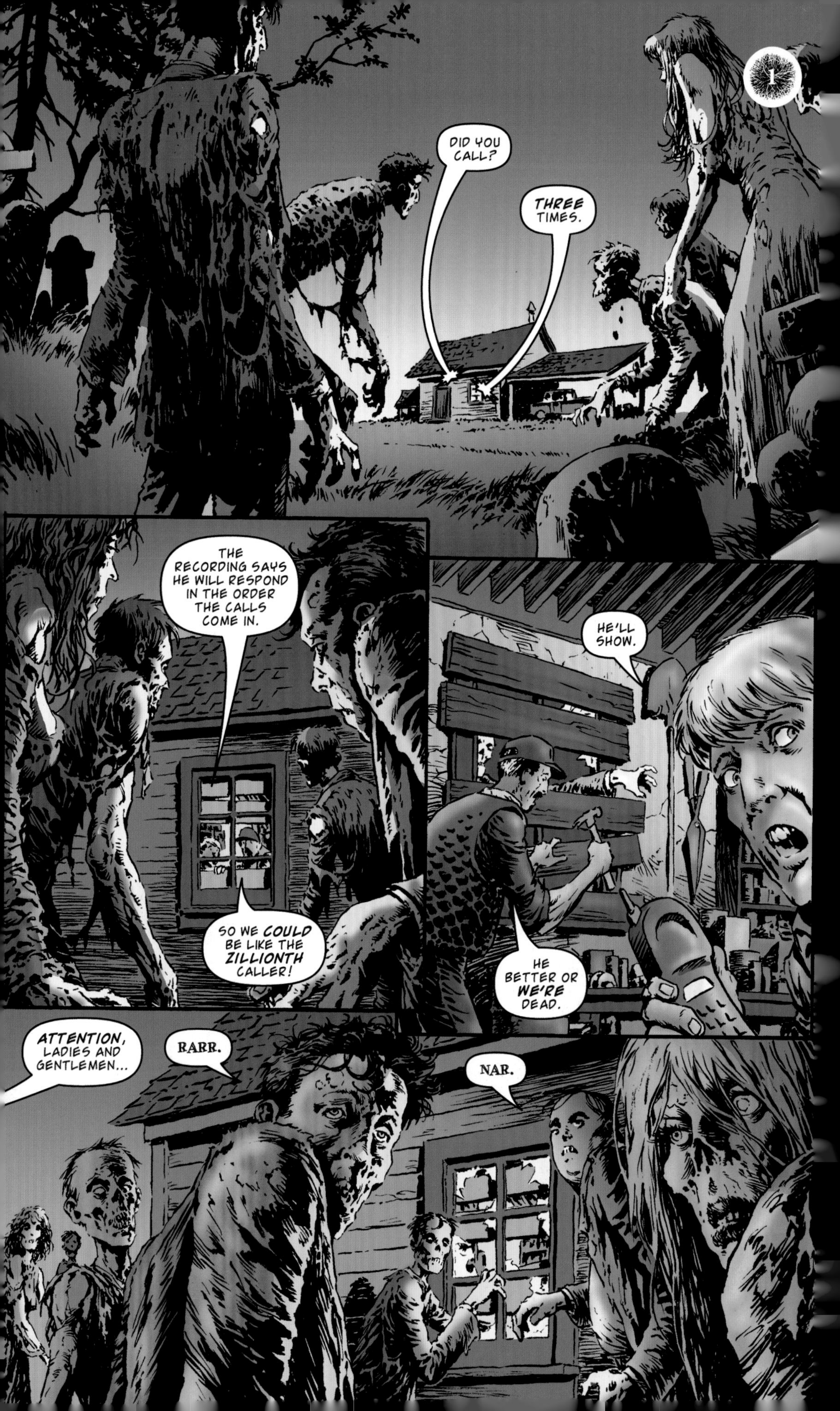

1
DID YOU CALL?
THREE TIMES.
THE RECORDING SAYS HE WILL RESPOND IN THE ORDER THE CALLS COME IN.
SO WE COULD BE LIKE THE ZILLIONTH CALLER!
HE'LL SHOW.
HE BETTER OR WE'RE DEAD.
ATTENTION, LADIES AND GENTLEMEN...
RARR.
NAR.

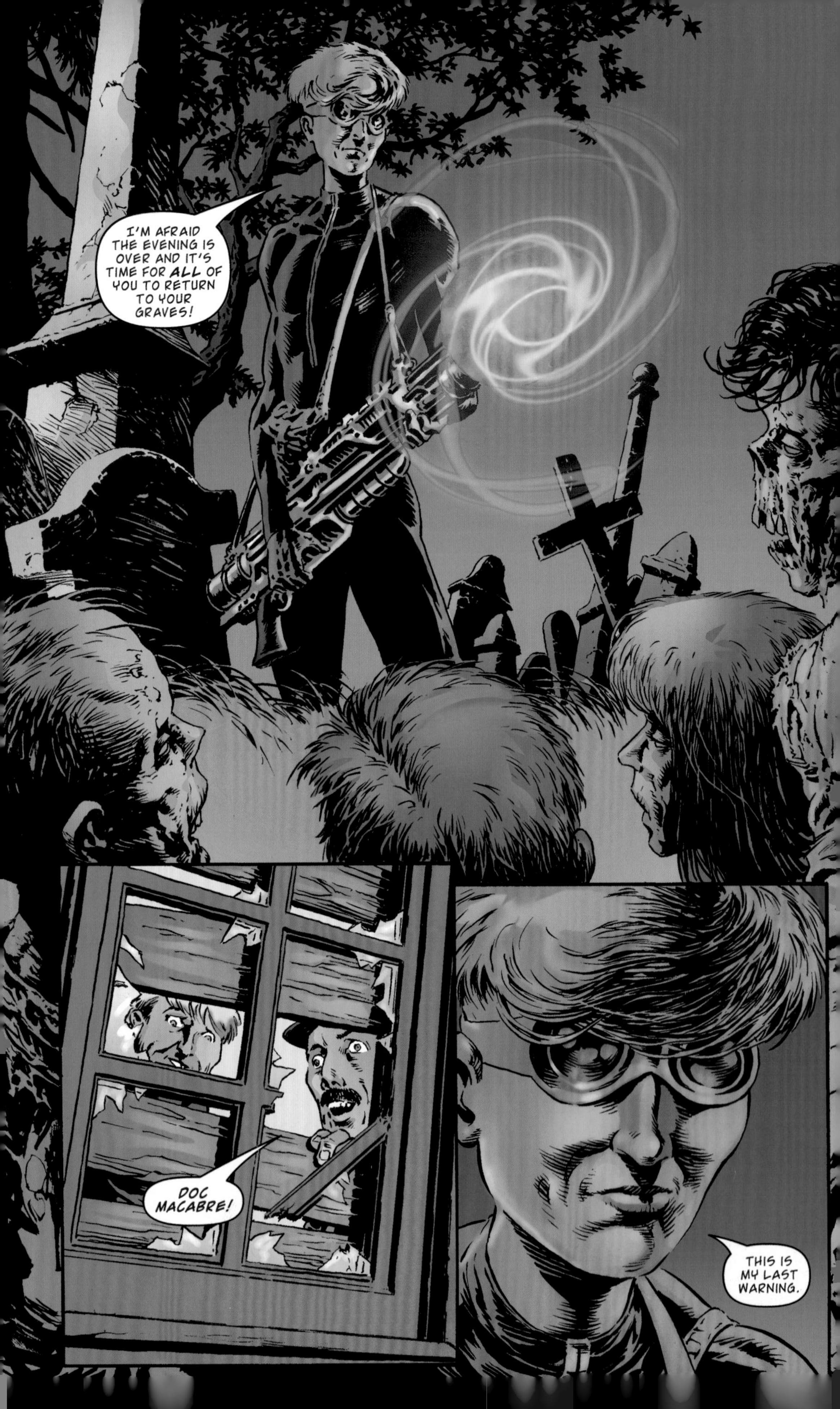
I'M AFRAID THE EVENING IS OVER AND IT'S TIME FOR ALL OF YOU TO RETURN TO YOUR GRAVES!
DOC MACABRE!
THIS IS MY LAST WARNING.

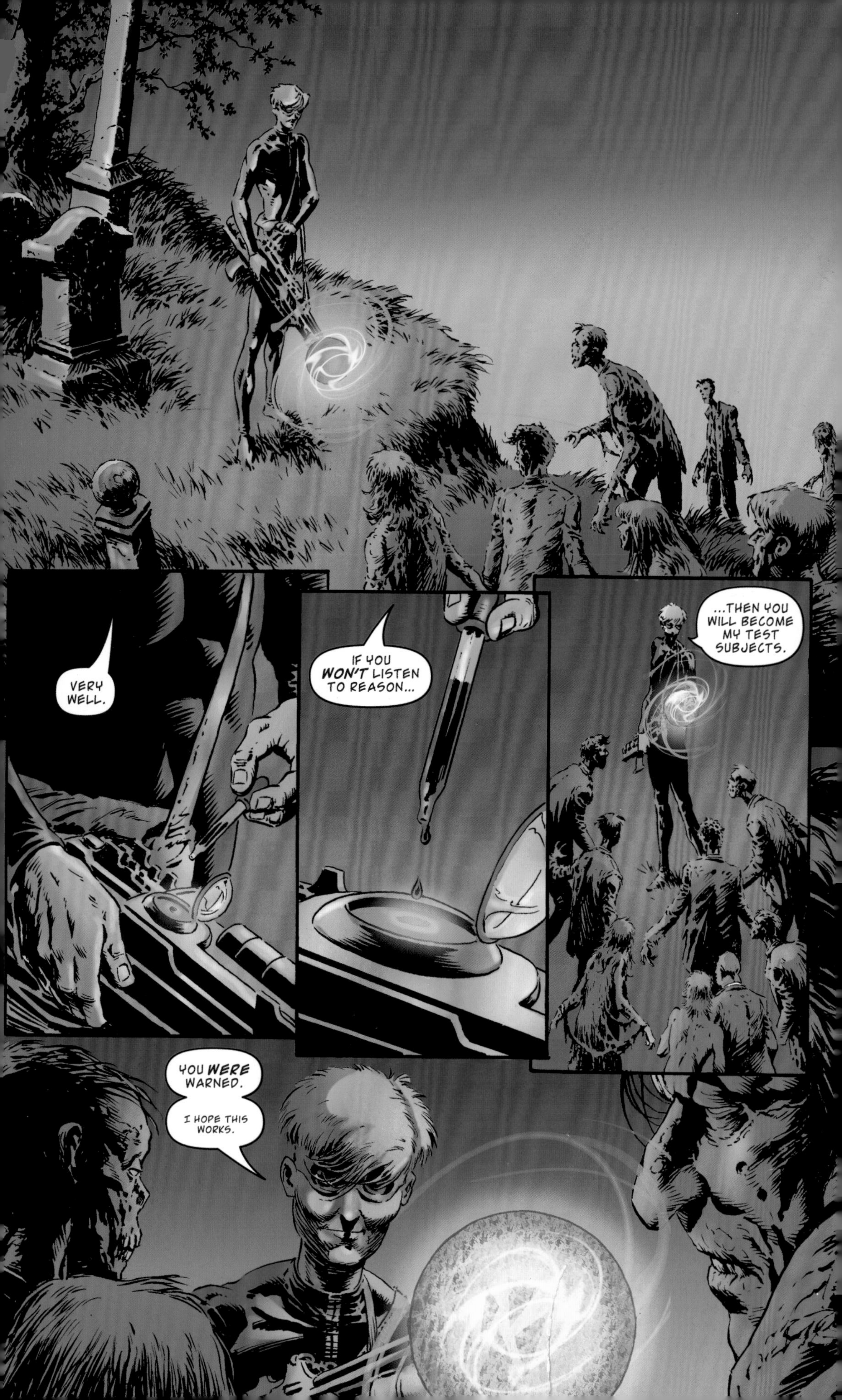
VERY WELL.
IF YOU WON'T LISTEN TO REASON...
...THEN YOU WILL BECOME MY TEST SUBJECTS.
YOU WERE WARNED.
I HOPE THIS WORKS.

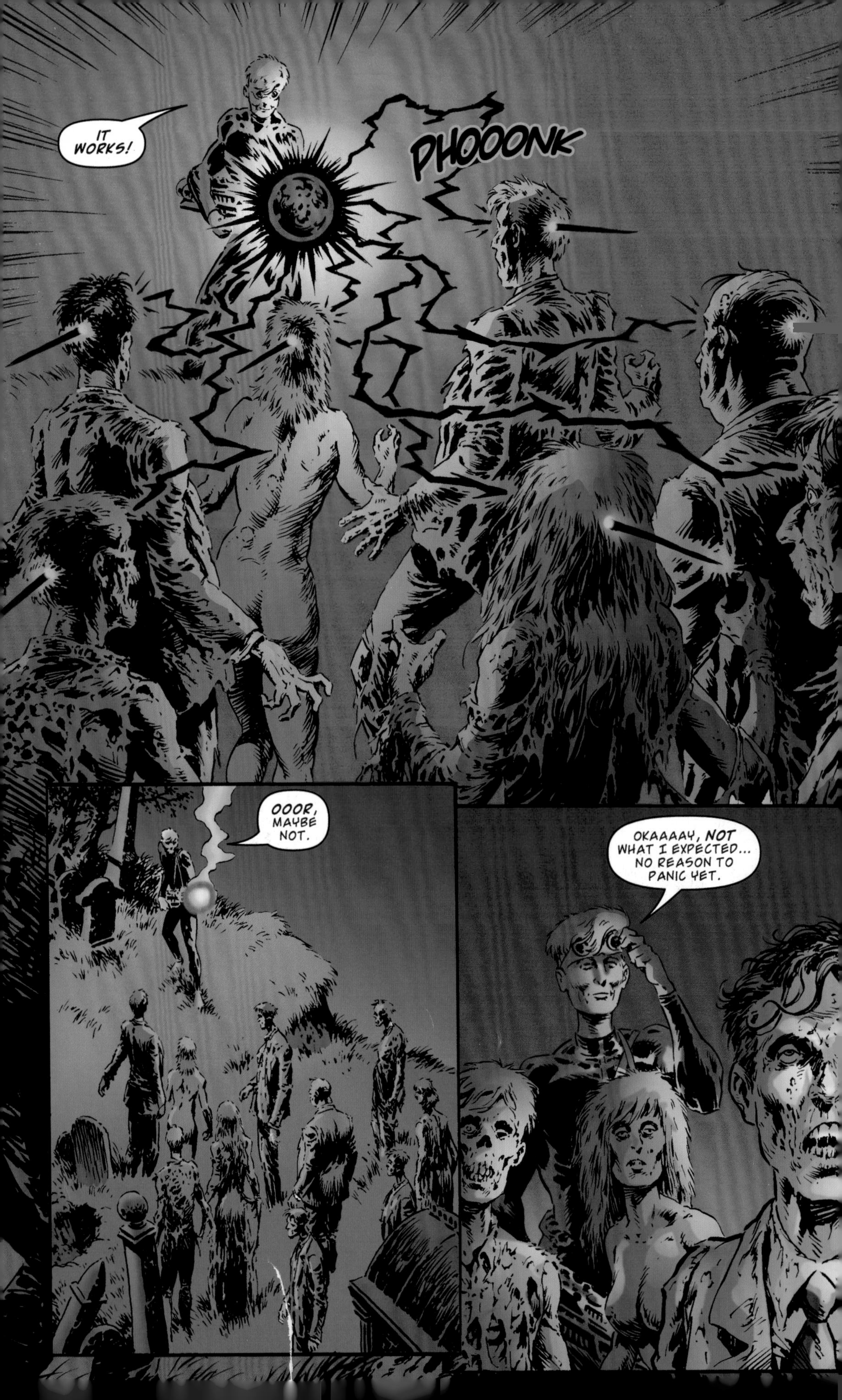
IT WORKS!
PHOOONK
OOOR, MAYBE NOT.
OKAAAAY, NOT WHAT I EXPECTED... NO REASON TO PANIC YET.

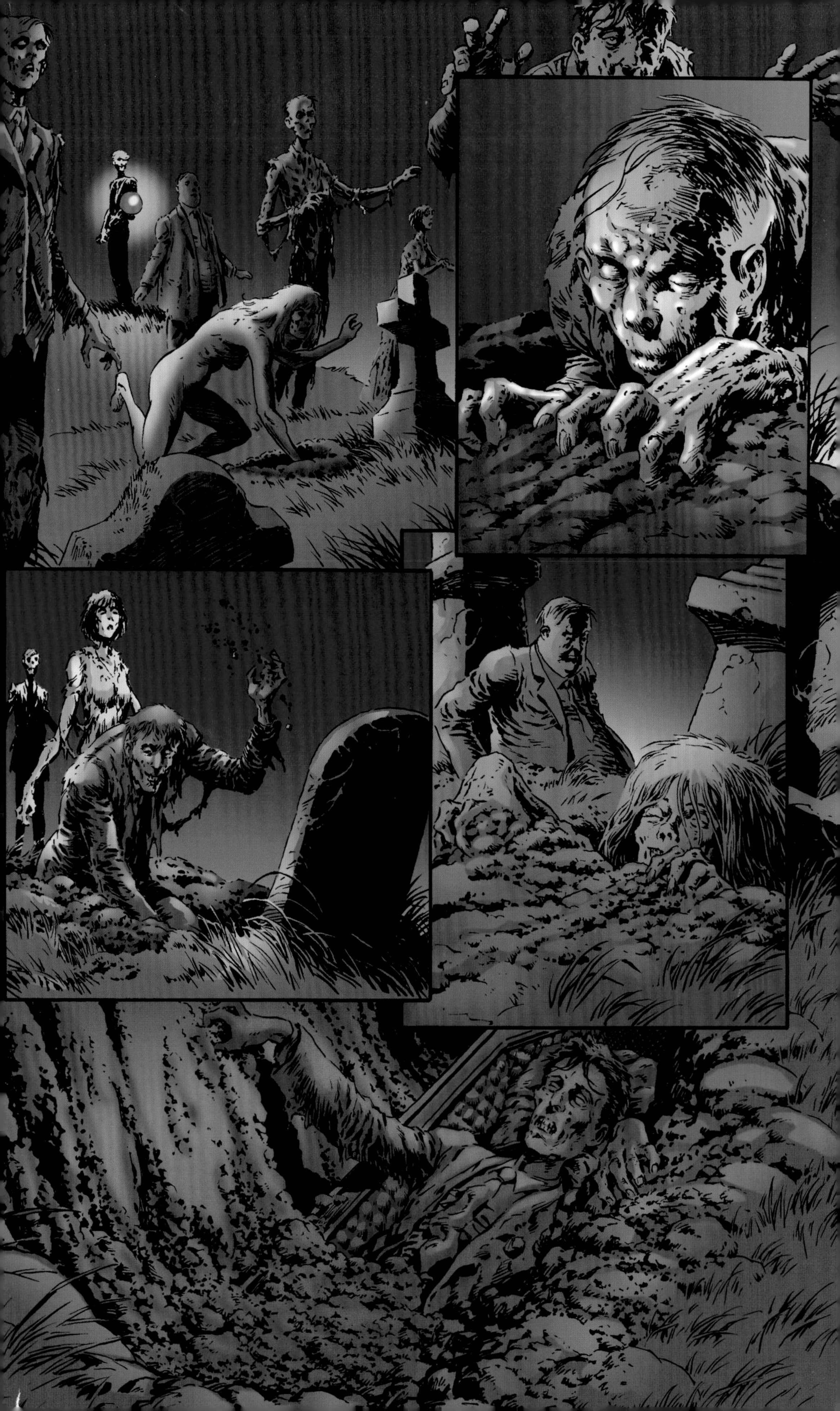

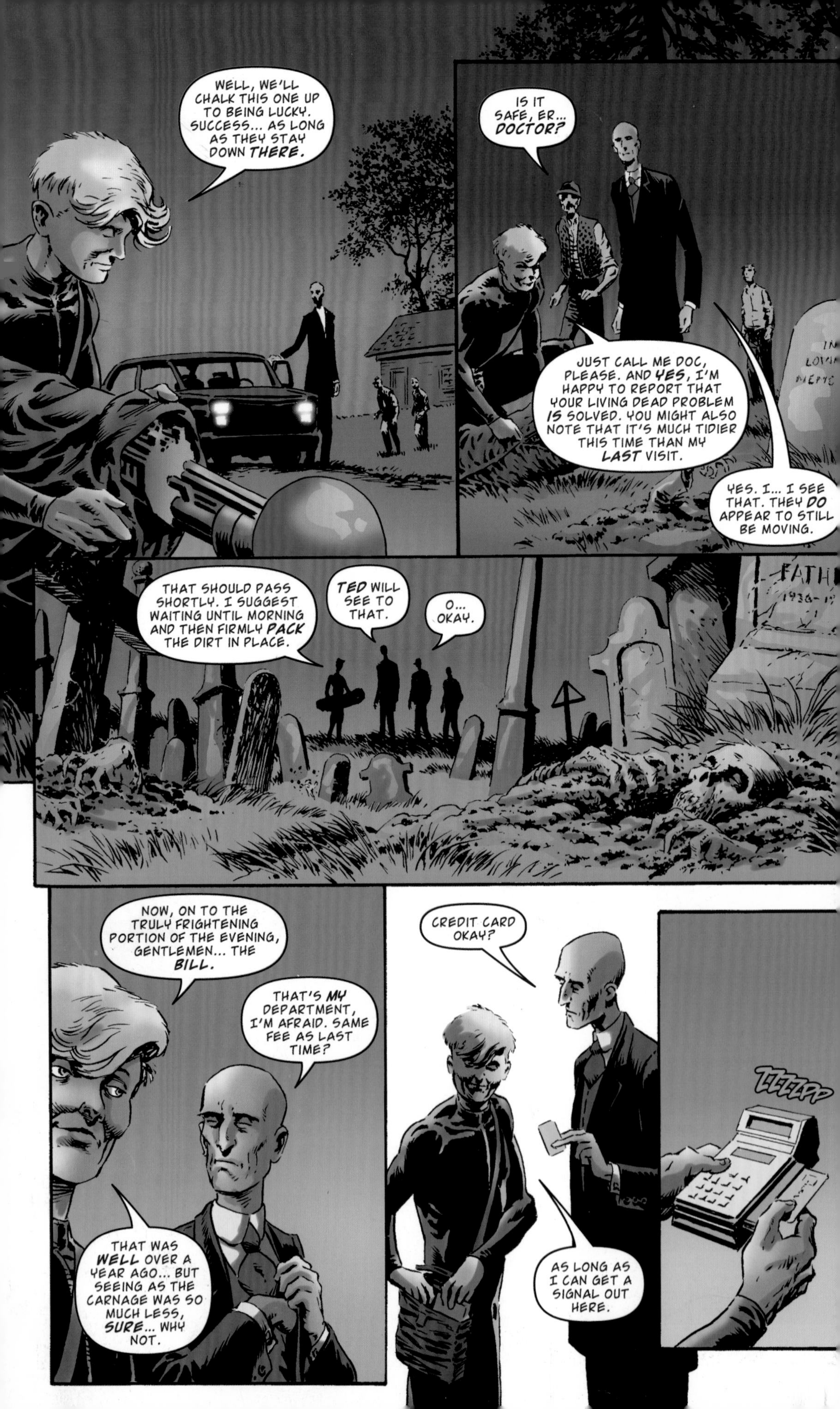
WELL, WE'LL CHALK THIS ONE UP TO BEING LUCKY. SUCCESS... AS LONG AS THEY STAY DOWN THERE.
IS IT SAFE, ER... DOCTOR?
JUST CALL ME DOC, PLEASE. AND YES, I'M HAPPY TO REPORT THAT YOUR LIVING DEAD PROBLEM IS SOLVED. YOU MIGHT ALSO NOTE THAT IT'S MUCH TIDIER THIS TIME THAN MY LAST VISIT.
YES. I... I SEE THAT. THEY DO APPEAR TO STILL BE MOVING.
THAT SHOULD PASS SHORTLY. I SUGGEST WAITING UNTIL MORNING AND THEN FIRMLY PACK THE DIRT IN PLACE.
TED WILL SEE TO THAT.
O... OKAY.
NOW, ON TO THE TRULY FRIGHTENING PORTION OF THE EVENING, GENTLEMEN... THE BILL.
THAT'S MY DEPARTMENT, I'M AFRAID. SAME FEE AS LAST TIME?
THAT WAS WELL OVER A YEAR AGO... BUT SEEING AS THE CARNAGE WAS SO MUCH LESS, SURE... WHY NOT.
CREDIT CARD OKAY?
AS LONG AS I CAN GET A SIGNAL OUT HERE.
TZZZAPP

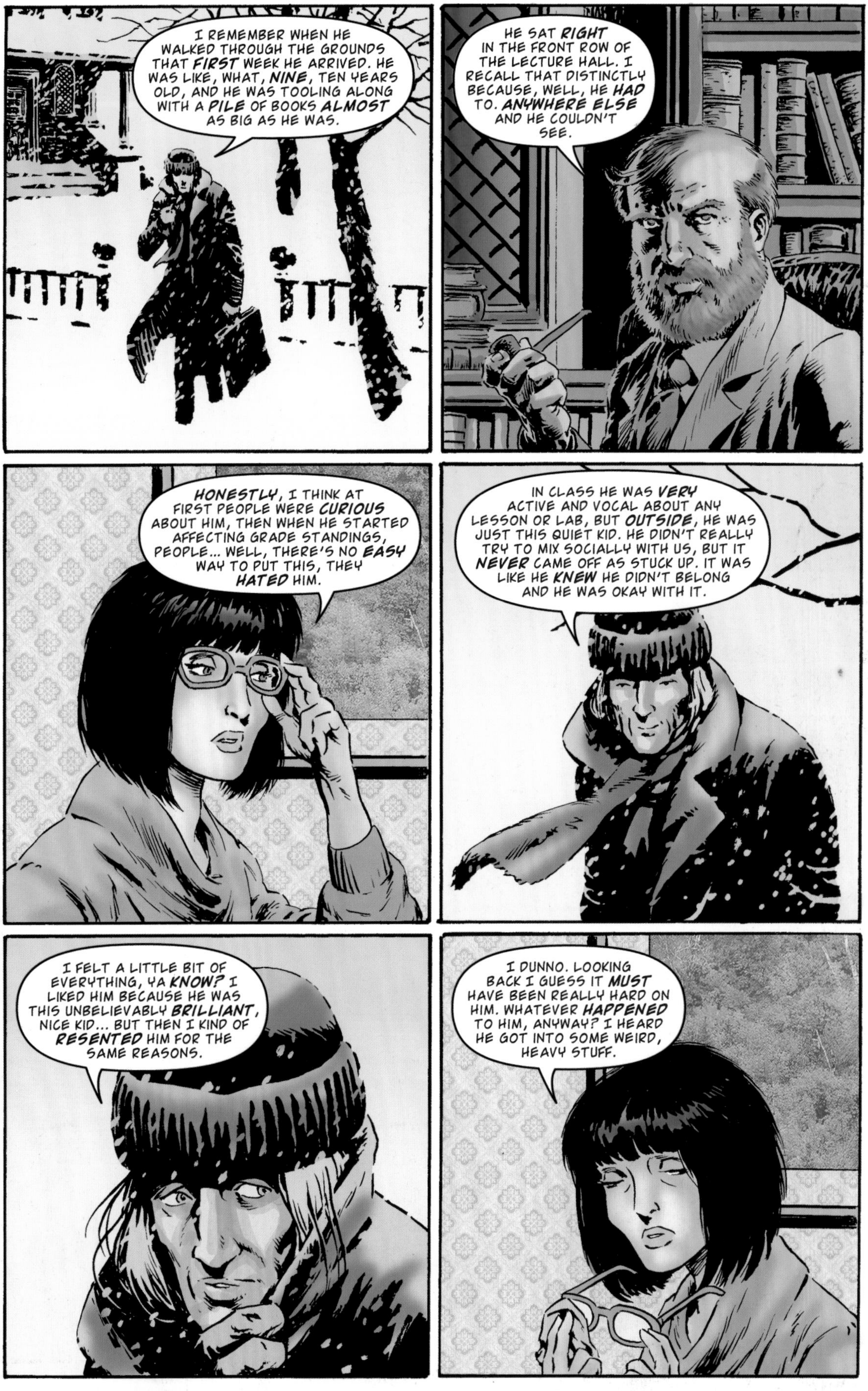
I REMEMBER WHEN HE WALKED THROUGH THE GROUNDS THAT FIRST WEEK HE ARRIVED. HE WAS LIKE, WHAT, NINE, TEN YEARS OLD, AND HE WAS TOOLING ALONG WITH A PILE OF BOOKS ALMOST AS BIG AS HE WAS.
HE SAT RIGHT IN THE FRONT ROW OF THE LECTURE HALL. I RECALL THAT DISTINCTLY BECAUSE, WELL, HE HAD TO. ANYWHERE ELSE AND HE COULDN'T SEE.
HONESTLY, I THINK AT FIRST PEOPLE WERE CURIOUS ABOUT HIM, THEN WHEN HE STARTED AFFECTING GRADE STANDINGS, PEOPLE... WELL, THERE'S NO EASY WAY TO PUT THIS, THEY HATED HIM.
IN CLASS HE WAS VERY ACTIVE AND VOCAL ABOUT ANY LESSON OR LAB, BUT OUTSIDE, HE WAS JUST THIS QUIET KID. HE DIDN'T REALLY TRY TO MIX SOCIALLY WITH US, BUT IT NEVER CAME OFF AS STUCK UP. IT WAS LIKE HE KNEW HE DIDN'T BELONG AND HE WAS OKAY WITH IT.
I FELT A LITTLE BIT OF EVERYTHING, YA KNOW? I LIKED HIM BECAUSE HE WAS THIS UNBELIEVABLY BRILLIANT, NICE KID... BUT THEN I KIND OF RESENTED HIM FOR THE SAME REASONS.
I DUNNO. LOOKING BACK I GUESS IT MUST HAVE BEEN REALLY HARD ON HIM. WHATEVER HAPPENED TO HIM, ANYWAY? I HEARD HE GOT INTO SOME WEIRD, HEAVY STUFF.

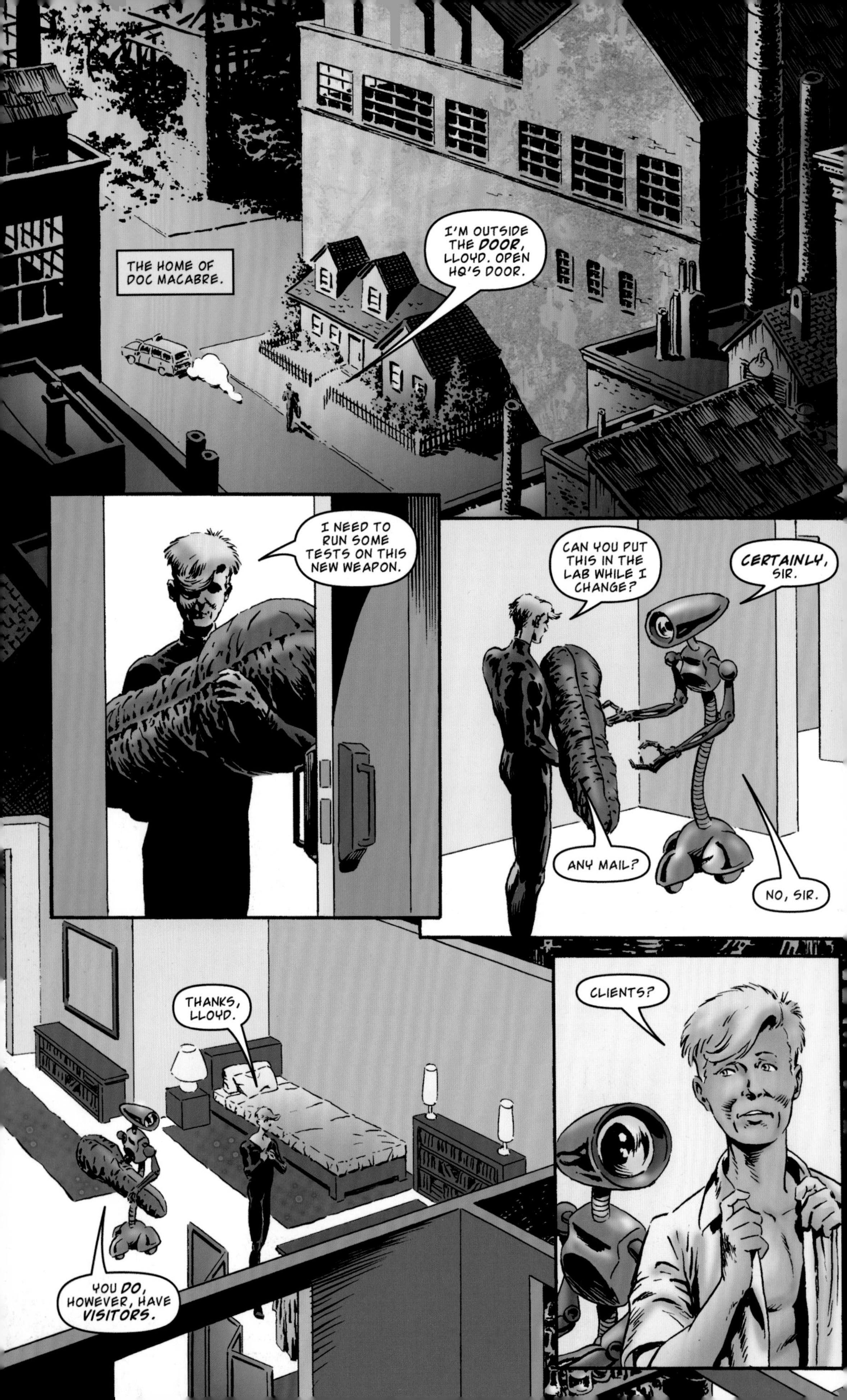
THE HOME OF DOC MACABRE.
I'M OUTSIDE THE DOOR, LLOYD. OPEN HQ'S DOOR.
I NEED TO RUN SOME TESTS ON THIS NEW WEAPON.
CAN YOU PUT THIS IN THE LAB WHILE I CHANGE?
CERTAINLY, SIR.
ANY MAIL?
NO, SIR.
THANKS, LLOYD.
YOU DO, HOWEVER, HAVE VISITORS.
CLIENTS?

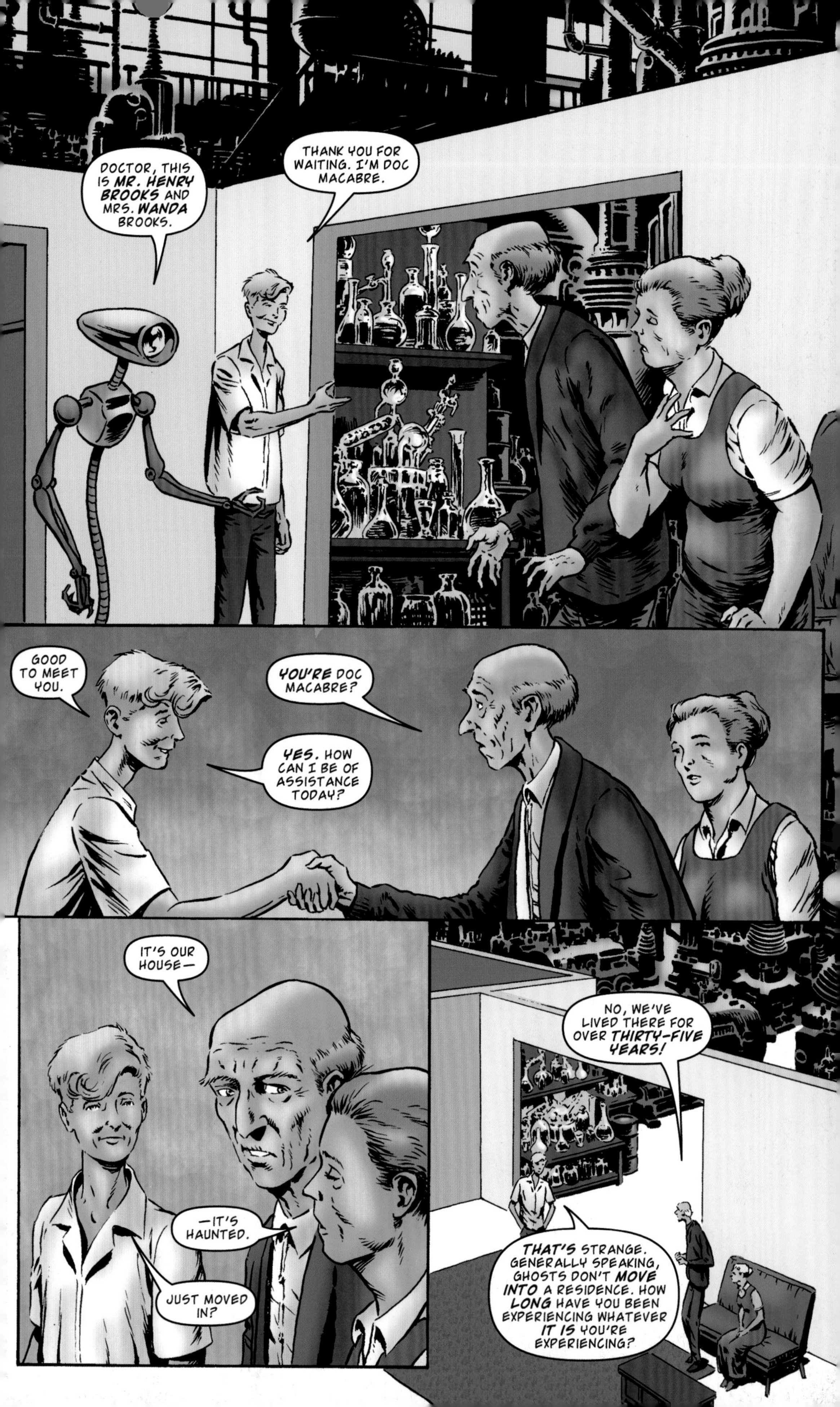

DOCTOR, THIS IS MR. HENRY BROOKS AND MRS. WANDA BROOKS.
THANK YOU FOR WAITING. I'M DOC MACABRE.
GOOD TO MEET YOU.
YOU'RE DOC MACABRE?
YES. HOW CAN I BE OF ASSISTANCE TODAY?
IT'S OUR HOUSE—
—IT'S HAUNTED.
JUST MOVED IN?
NO, WE'VE LIVED THERE FOR OVER THIRTY-FIVE YEARS!
THAT'S STRANGE. GENERALLY SPEAKING, GHOSTS DON'T MOVE INTO A RESIDENCE. HOW LONG HAVE YOU BEEN EXPERIENCING WHATEVER IT IS YOU'RE EXPERIENCING?

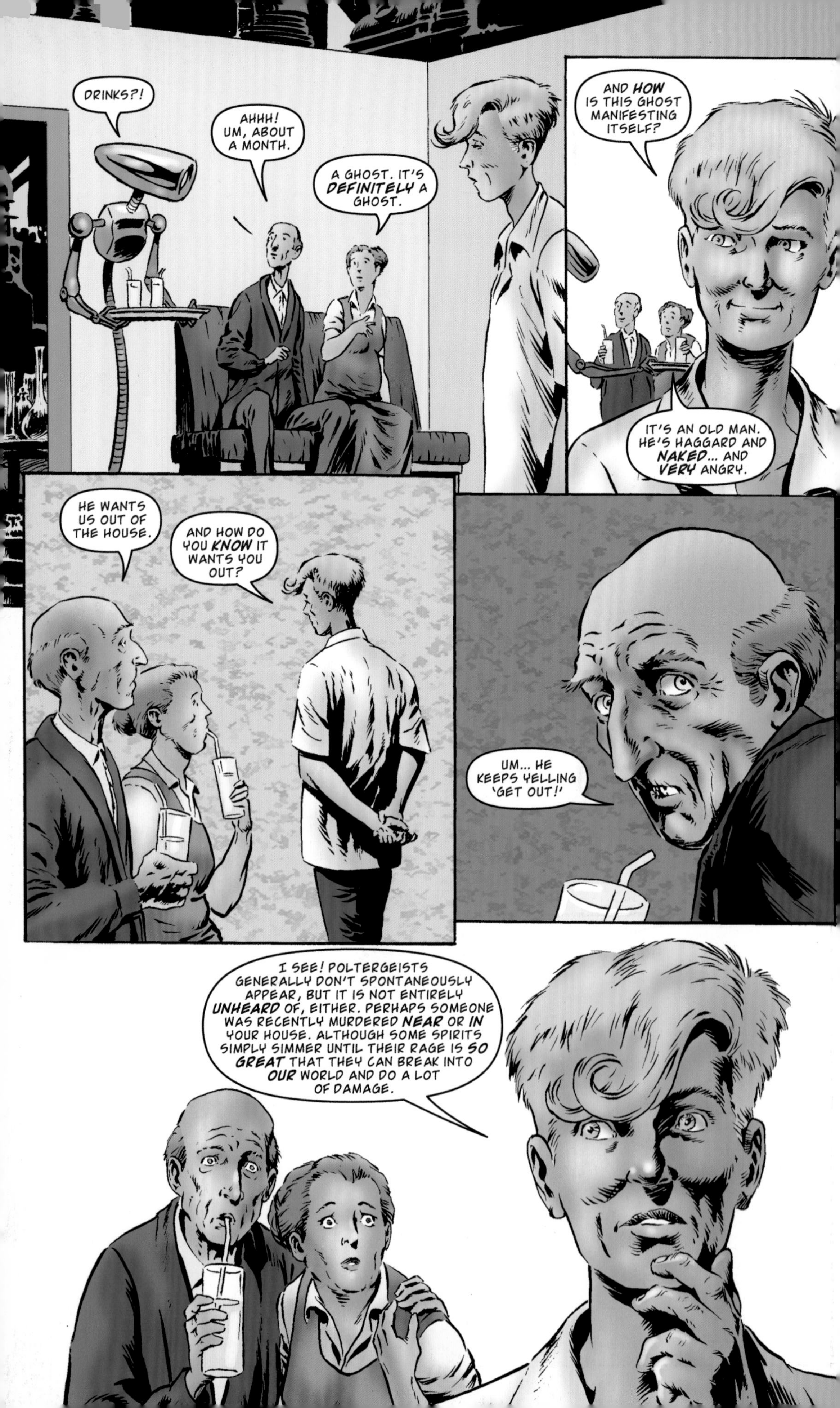
DRINKS?!
AHHH! UM, ABOUT A MONTH.
A GHOST. IT'S DEFINITELY A GHOST.
AND HOW IS THIS GHOST MANIFESTING ITSELF?
IT'S AN OLD MAN. HE'S HAGGARD AND NAKED... AND VERY ANGRY.
HE WANTS US OUT OF THE HOUSE.
AND HOW DO YOU KNOW IT WANTS YOU OUT?
UM... HE KEEPS YELLING 'GET OUT!'
I SEE! POLTERGEISTS GENERALLY DON'T SPONTANEOUSLY APPEAR, BUT IT IS NOT ENTIRELY UNHEARD OF, EITHER. PERHAPS SOMEONE WAS RECENTLY MURDERED NEAR OR IN YOUR HOUSE. ALTHOUGH SOME SPIRITS SIMPLY SIMMER UNTIL THEIR RAGE IS SO GREAT THAT THEY CAN BREAK INTO OUR WORLD AND DO A LOT OF DAMAGE.

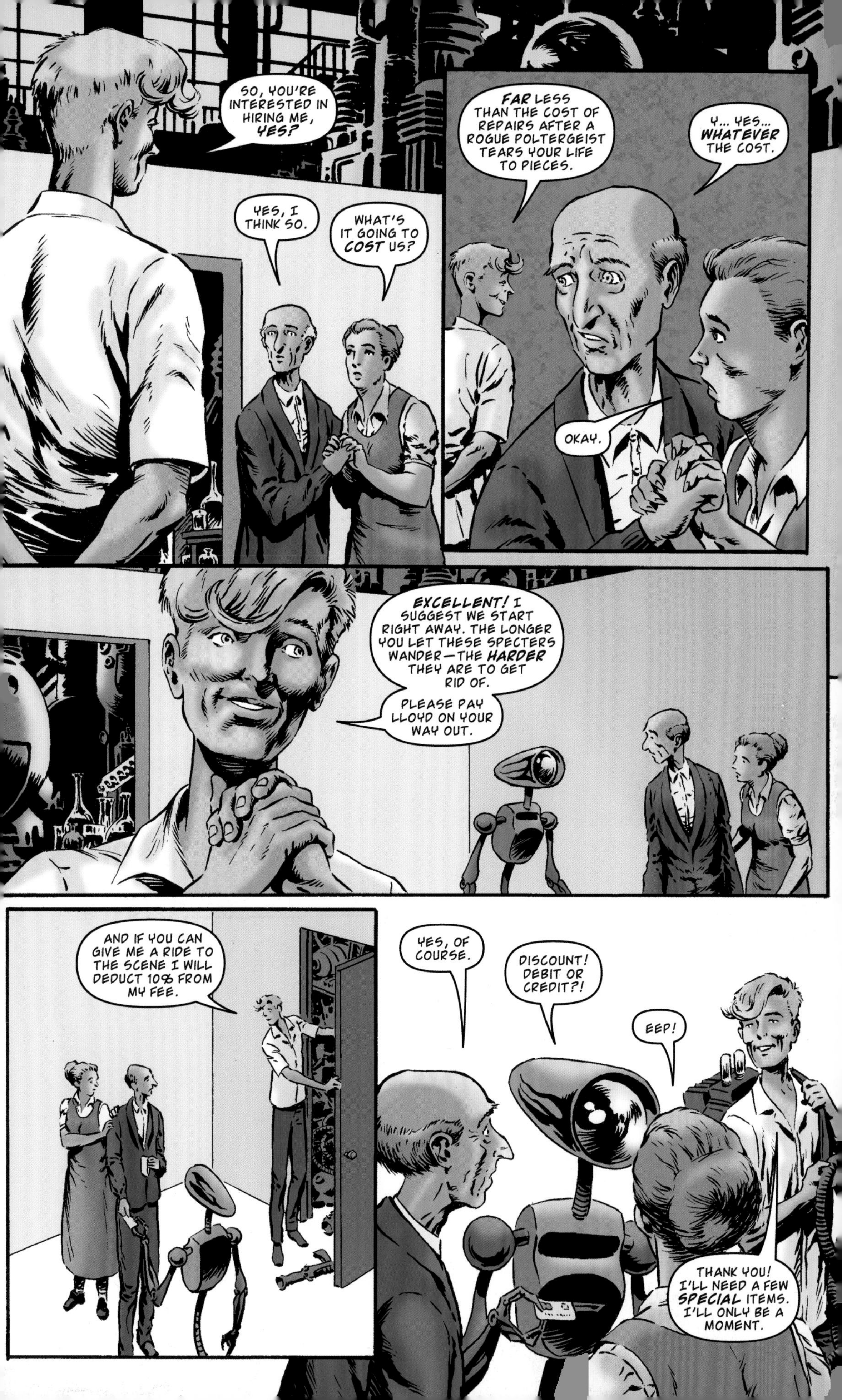
SO, YOU'RE INTERESTED IN HIRING ME, YES?
YES, I THINK SO.
WHAT'S IT GOING TO COST US?
FAR LESS THAN THE COST OF REPAIRS AFTER A ROGUE POLTERGEIST TEARS YOUR LIFE TO PIECES.
Y... YES... WHATEVER THE COST.
OKAY.
EXCELLENT! I SUGGEST WE START RIGHT AWAY. THE LONGER YOU LET THESE SPECTERS WANDER—THE HARDER THEY ARE TO GET RID OF.
PLEASE PAY LLOYD ON YOUR WAY OUT.
AND IF YOU CAN GIVE ME A RIDE TO THE SCENE I WILL DEDUCT 10% FROM MY FEE.
YES, OF COURSE.
DISCOUNT! DEBIT OR CREDIT?!
EEP!
THANK YOU! I'LL NEED A FEW SPECIAL ITEMS. I'LL ONLY BE A MOMENT.

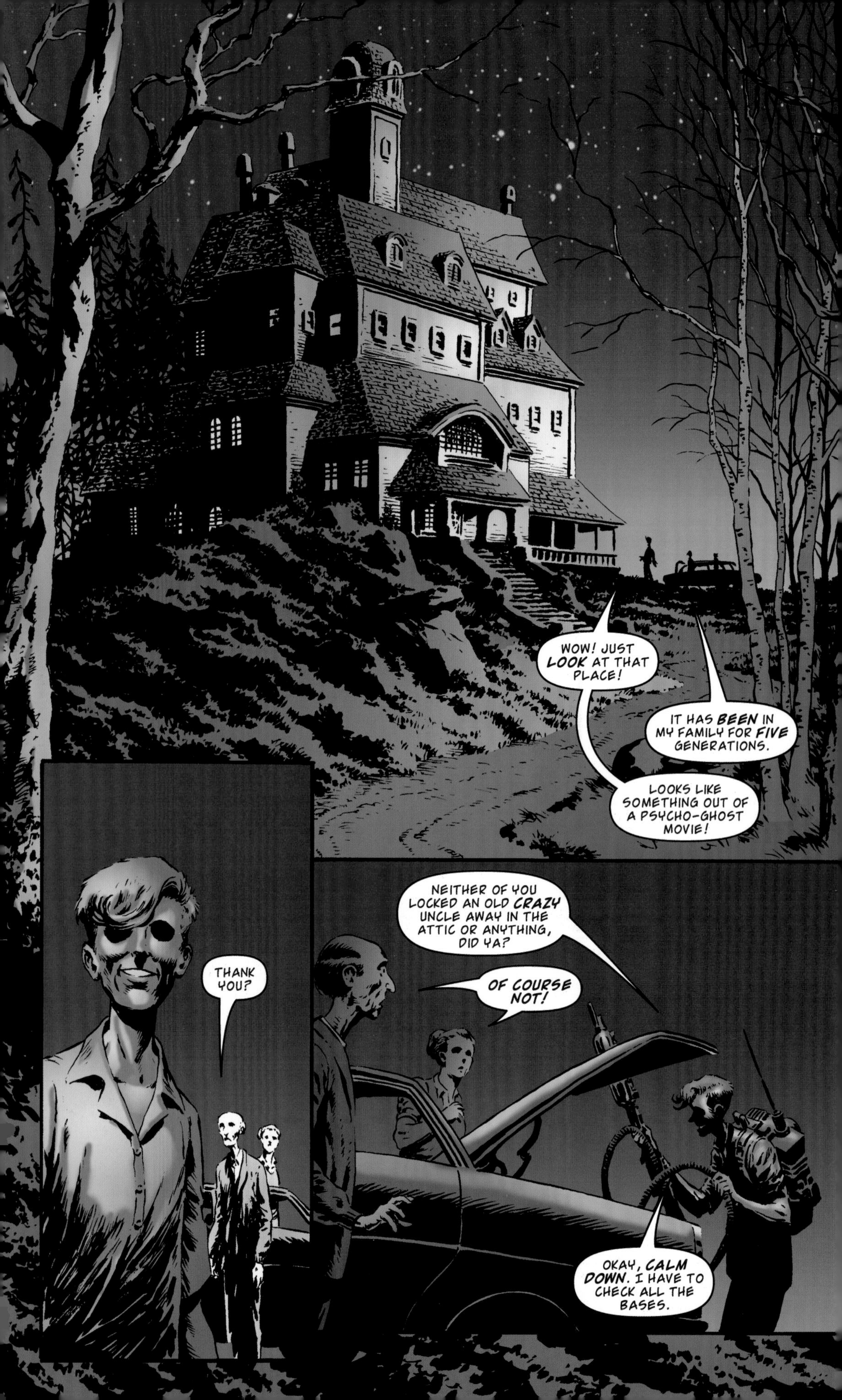

WOW! JUST LOOK AT THAT PLACE!
IT HAS BEEN IN MY FAMILY FOR FIVE GENERATIONS.
LOOKS LIKE SOMETHING OUT OF A PSYCHO-GHOST MOVIE!
THANK YOU?
NEITHER OF YOU LOCKED AN OLD CRAZY UNCLE AWAY IN THE ATTIC OR ANYTHING, DID YA?
OF COURSE NOT!
OKAY, CALM DOWN. I HAVE TO CHECK ALL THE BASES.

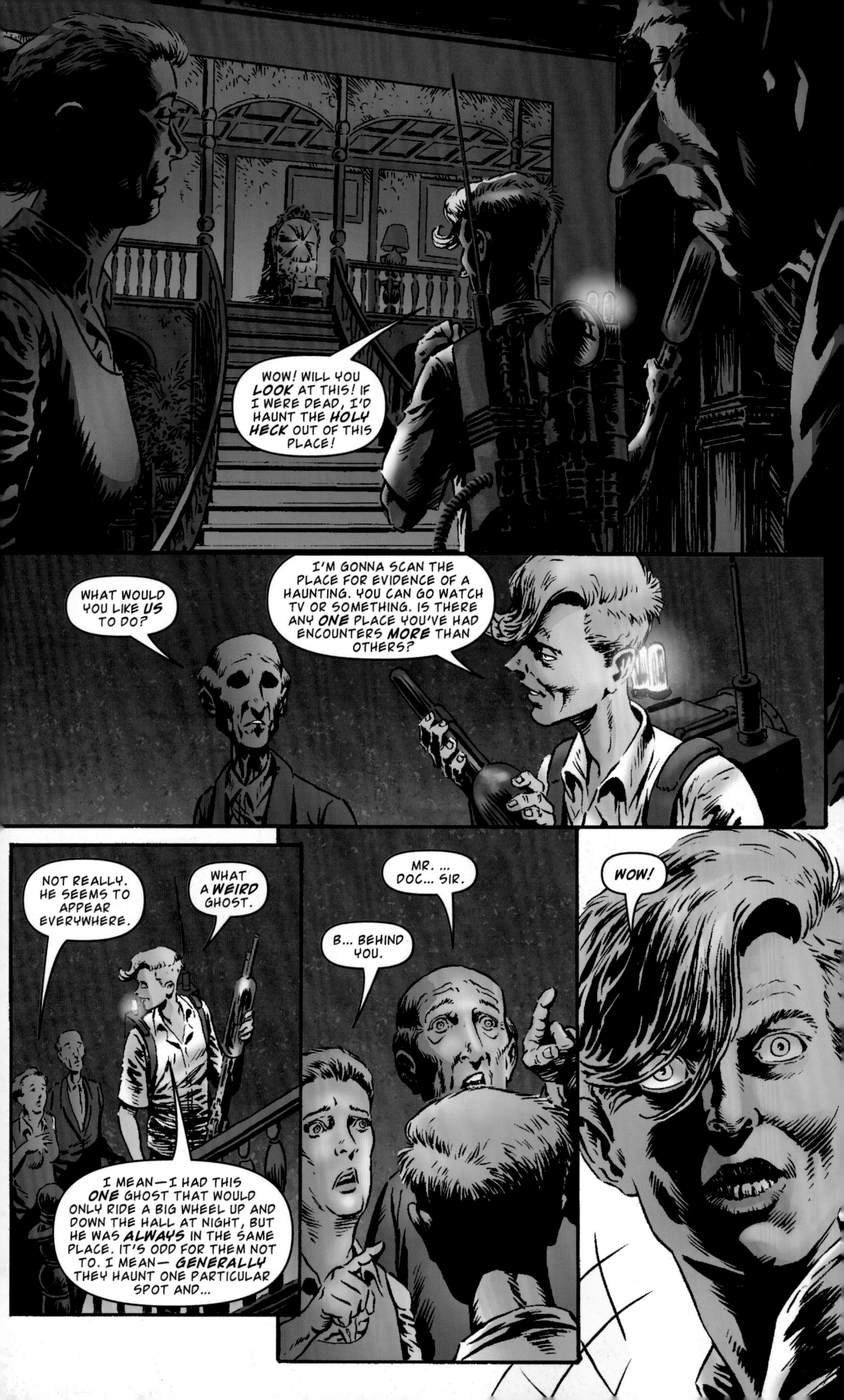
WOW! WILL YOU LOOK AT THIS! IF I WERE DEAD, I'D HAUNT THE HOLY HECK OUT OF THIS PLACE!
WHAT WOULD YOU LIKE US TO DO?
I'M GONNA SCAN THE PLACE FOR EVIDENCE OF A HAUNTING. YOU CAN GO WATCH TV OR SOMETHING. IS THERE ANY ONE PLACE YOU'VE HAD ENCOUNTERS MORE THAN OTHERS?
NOT REALLY. HE SEEMS TO APPEAR EVERYWHERE.
WHAT A WEIRD GHOST.
I MEAN—I HAD THIS ONE GHOST THAT WOULD ONLY RIDE A BIG WHEEL UP AND DOWN THE HALL AT NIGHT, BUT HE WAS ALWAYS IN THE SAME PLACE. IT'S ODD FOR THEM NOT TO. I MEAN— GENERALLY THEY HAUNT ONE PARTICULAR SPOT AND...
MR. ... DOC... SIR.
B... BEHIND YOU.
WOW!

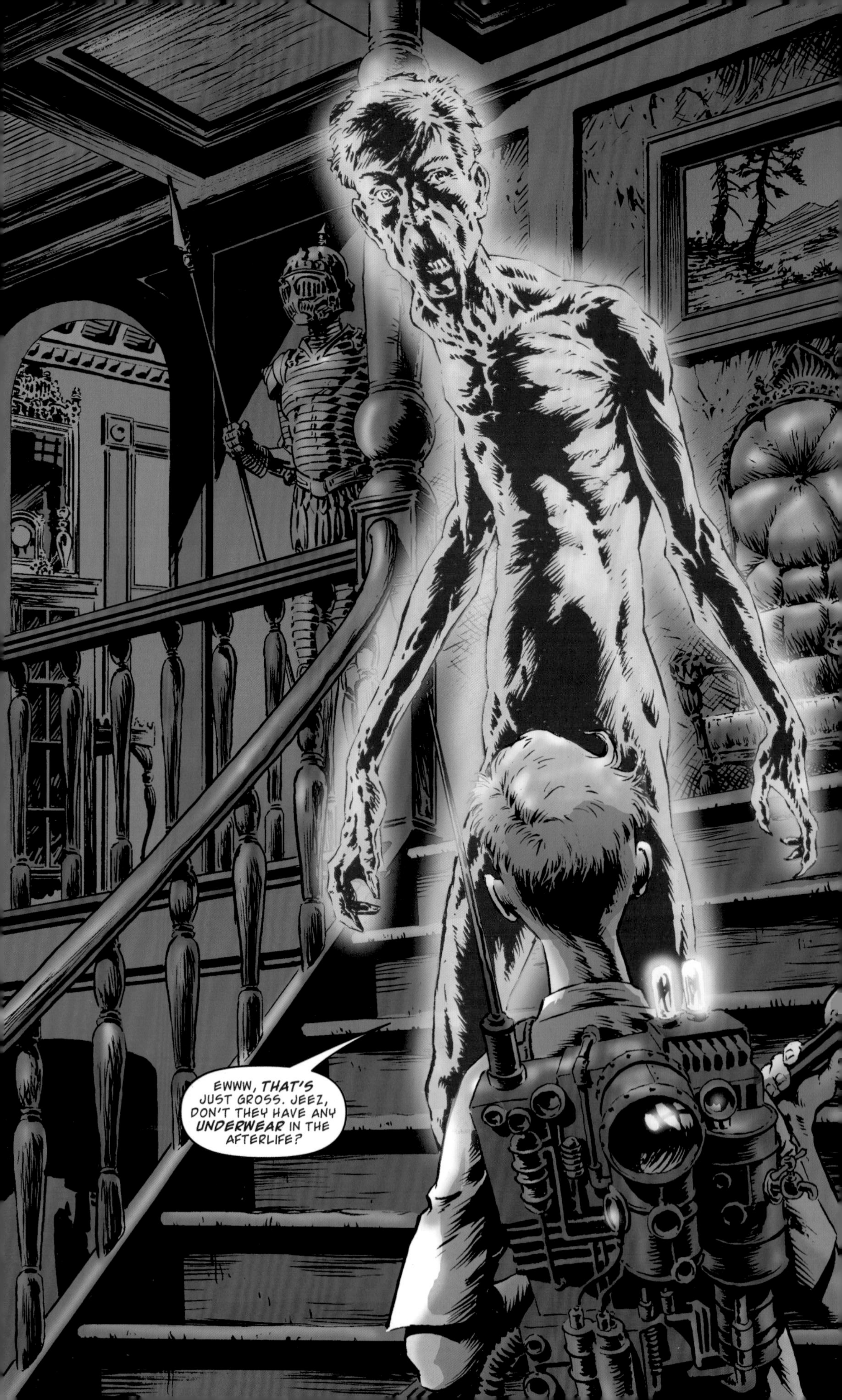
EWWW, THAT'S JUST GROSS. JEEZ, DON'T THEY HAVE ANY UNDERWEAR IN THE AFTERLIFE?

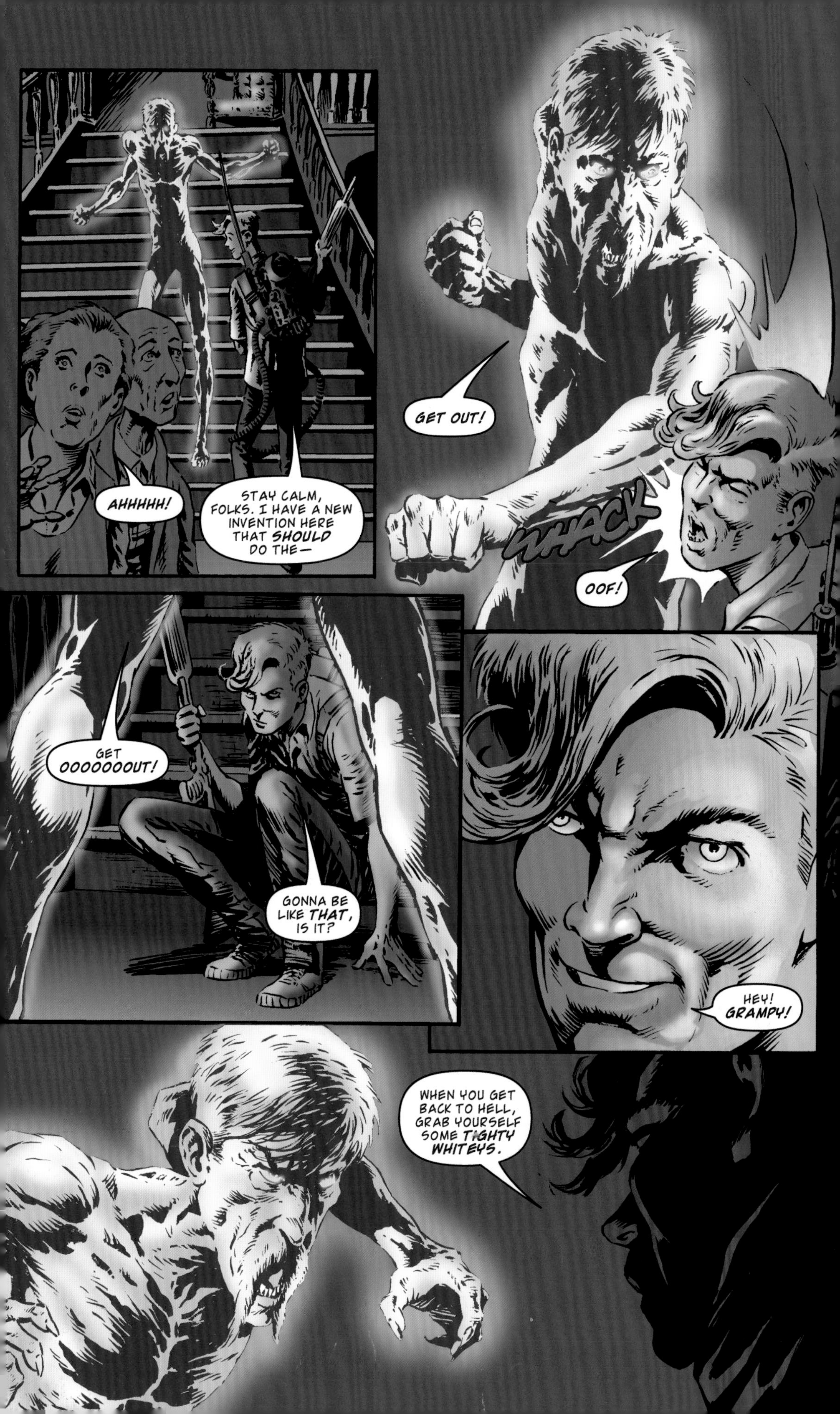
AHHHHH!
STAY CALM, FOLKS. I HAVE A NEW INVENTION HERE THAT SHOULD DO THE—
GET OUT!
WHACK
OOF!
GET OOOOOOOUT!
GONNA BE LIKE THAT, IS IT?
HEY! GRAMPY!
WHEN YOU GET BACK TO HELL, GRAB YOURSELF SOME TIGHTY WHITEYS.

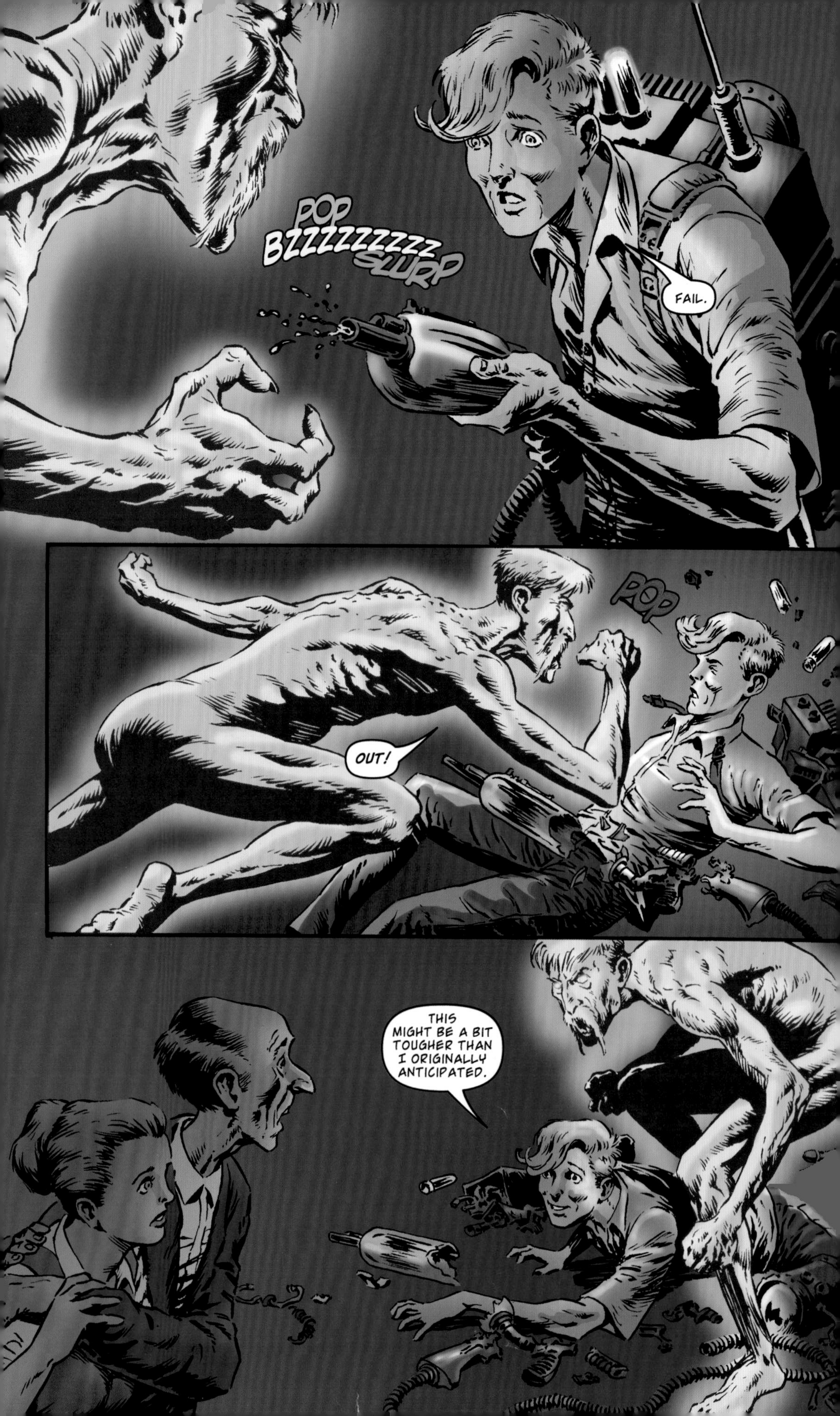
POP
BZZZZZZZZZZ
SLURP
FAIL.
POP
OUT!
THIS MIGHT BE A BIT TOUGHER THAN I ORIGINALLY ANTICIPATED.

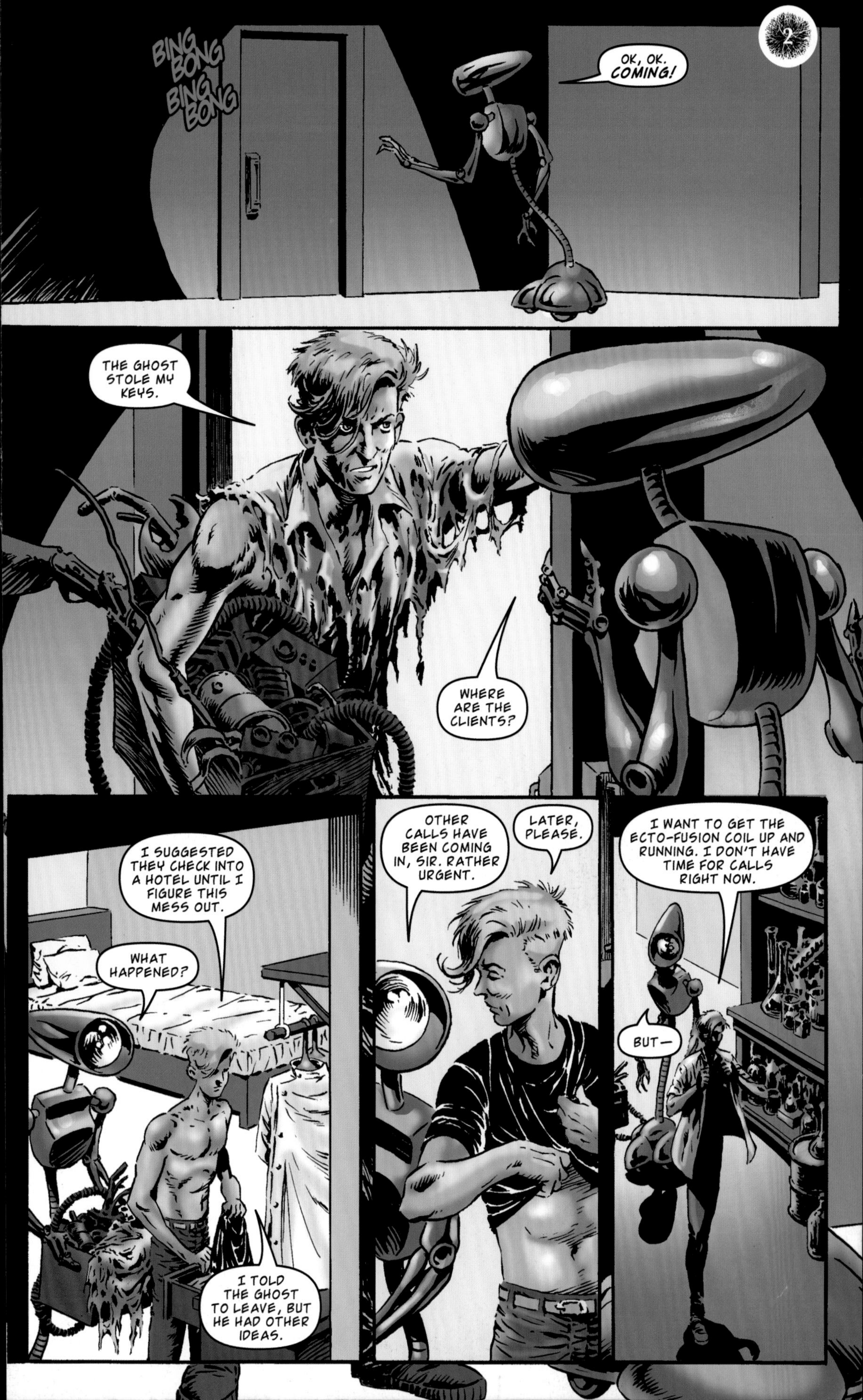
BING BONG BING BONG
OK, OK. COMING!
THE GHOST STOLE MY KEYS.
WHERE ARE THE CLIENTS?
I SUGGESTED THEY CHECK INTO A HOTEL UNTIL I FIGURE THIS MESS OUT.
WHAT HAPPENED?
I TOLD THE GHOST TO LEAVE, BUT HE HAD OTHER IDEAS.
OTHER CALLS HAVE BEEN COMING IN, SIR. RATHER URGENT.
LATER, PLEASE.
I WANT TO GET THE ECTO-FUSION COIL UP AND RUNNING. I DON'T HAVE TIME FOR CALLS RIGHT NOW.
BUT—

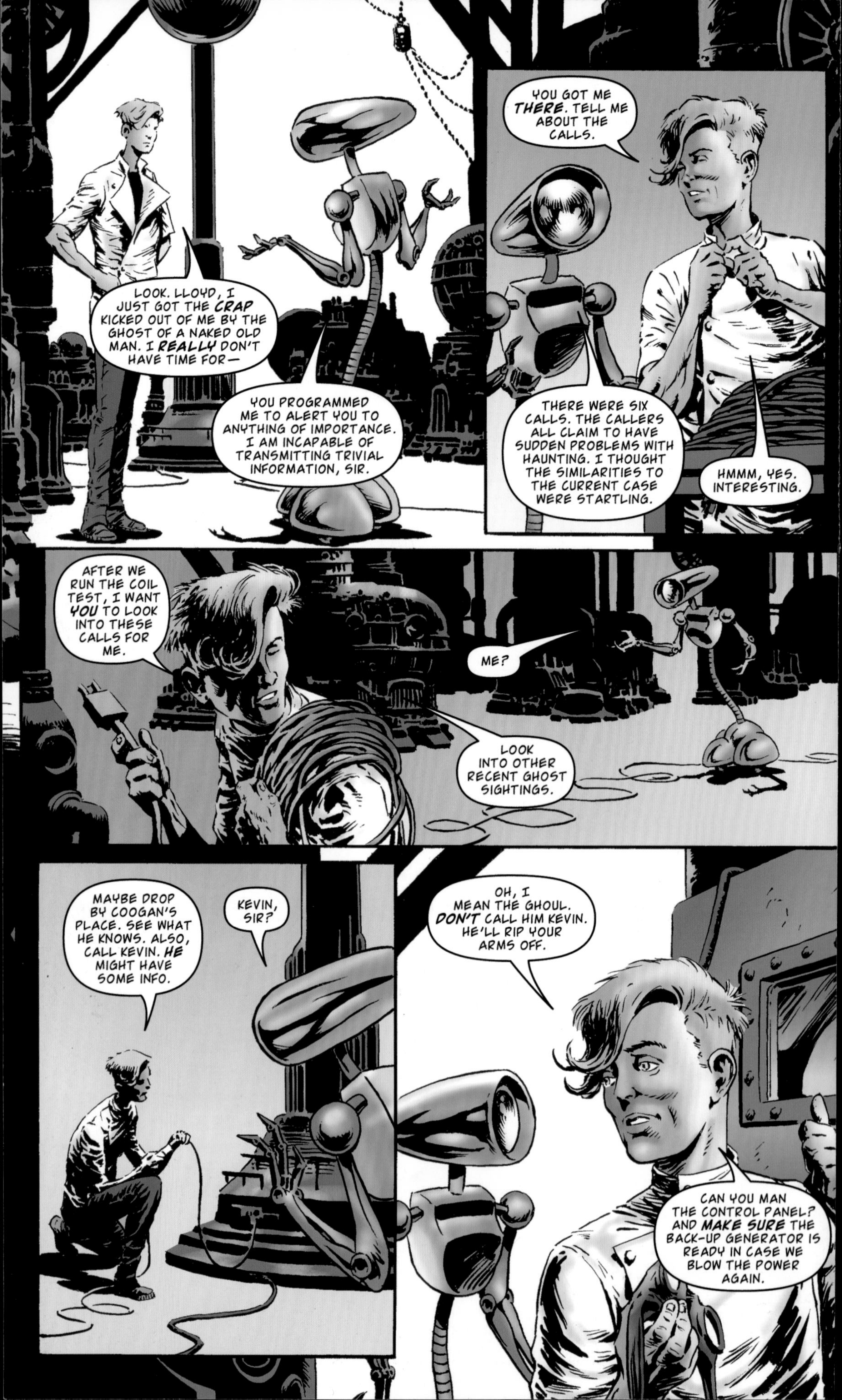
LOOK. LLOYD, I JUST GOT THE CRAP KICKED OUT OF ME BY THE GHOST OF A NAKED OLD MAN. I REALLY DON'T HAVE TIME FOR—
YOU PROGRAMMED ME TO ALERT YOU TO ANYTHING OF IMPORTANCE. I AM INCAPABLE OF TRANSMITTING TRIVIAL INFORMATION, SIR.
YOU GOT ME THERE. TELL ME ABOUT THE CALLS.
THERE WERE SIX CALLS. THE CALLERS ALL CLAIM TO HAVE SUDDEN PROBLEMS WITH HAUNTING. I THOUGHT THE SIMILARITIES TO THE CURRENT CASE WERE STARTLING.
HMMM, YES. INTERESTING.
AFTER WE RUN THE COIL TEST, I WANT YOU TO LOOK INTO THESE CALLS FOR ME.
ME?
LOOK INTO OTHER RECENT GHOST SIGHTINGS.
MAYBE DROP BY COOGAN'S PLACE. SEE WHAT HE KNOWS. ALSO, CALL KEVIN. HE MIGHT HAVE SOME INFO.
KEVIN, SIR?
OH, I MEAN THE GHOUL. DON'T CALL HIM KEVIN. HE'LL RIP YOUR ARMS OFF.
CAN YOU MAN THE CONTROL PANEL? AND MAKE SURE THE BACK-UP GENERATOR IS READY IN CASE WE BLOW THE POWER AGAIN.

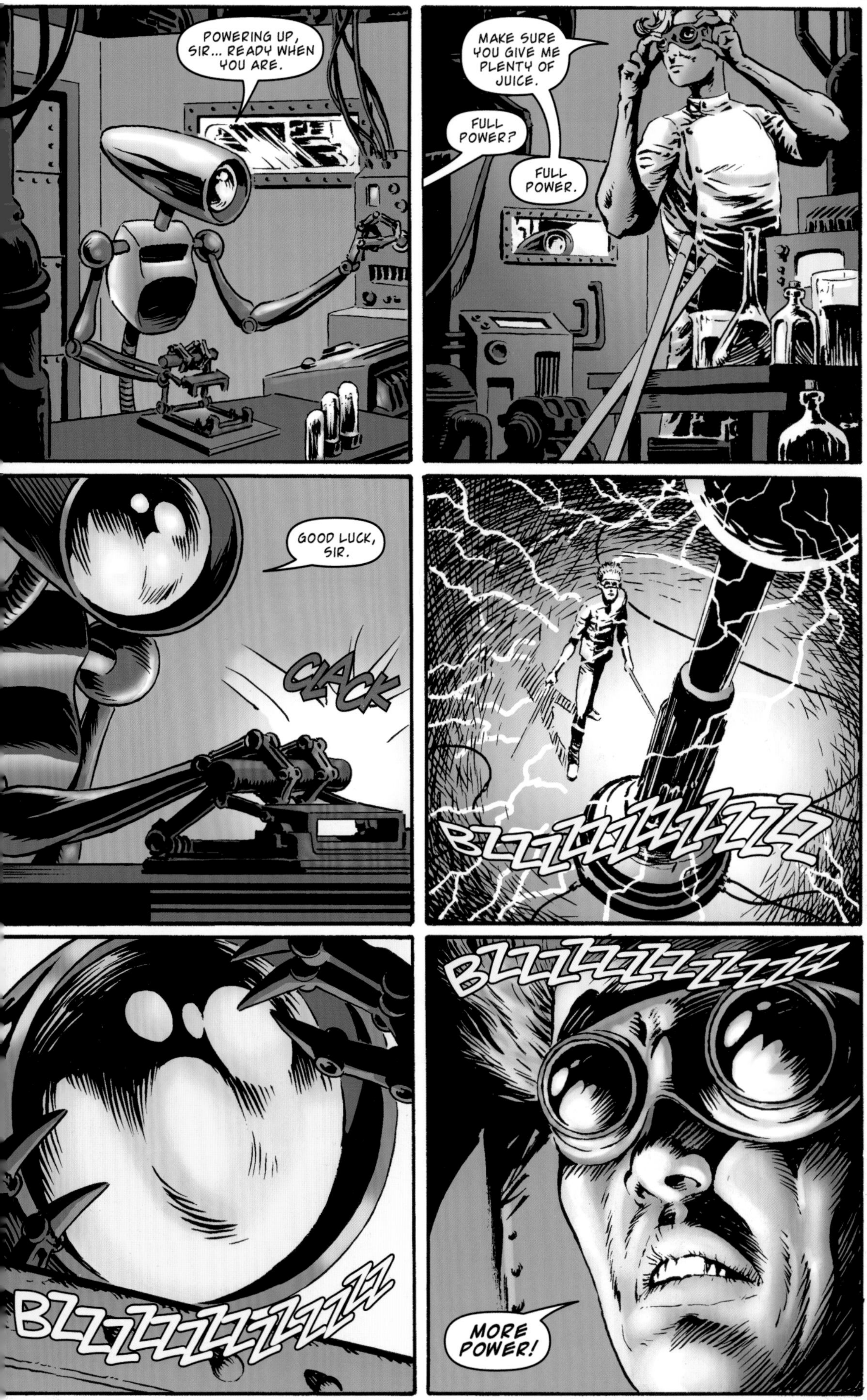

POWERING UP, SIR... READY WHEN YOU ARE.
MAKE SURE YOU GIVE ME PLENTY OF JUICE.
FULL POWER?
FULL POWER.
GOOD LUCK, SIR.
CLACK
BZZZZZZZZZZZZZ
BZZZZZZZZZZZZZZZ
BZZZZZZZZZZZZZZZ
MORE POWER!

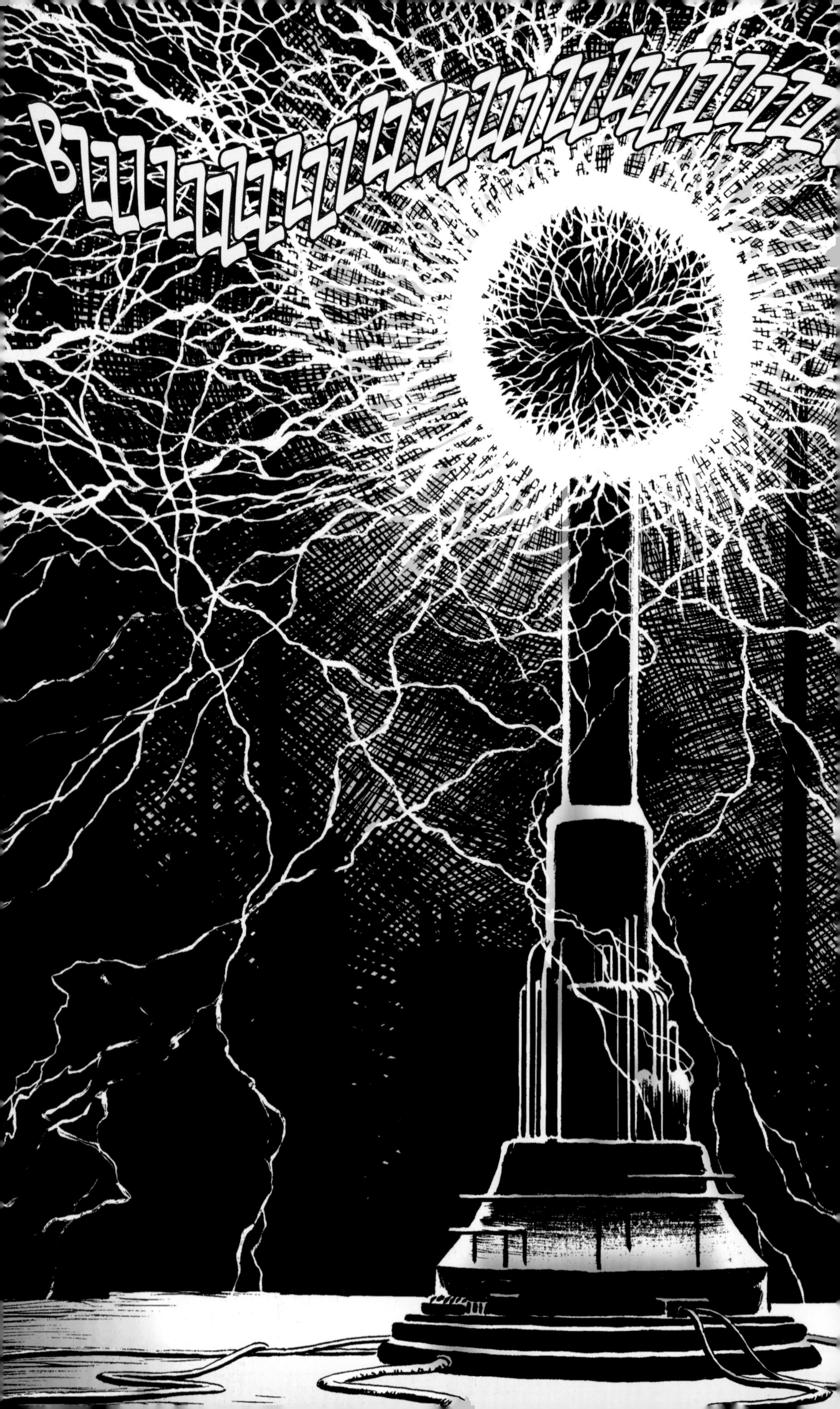

BZZZZZZZZZZZZZZZZZZZZZZZZZZZ

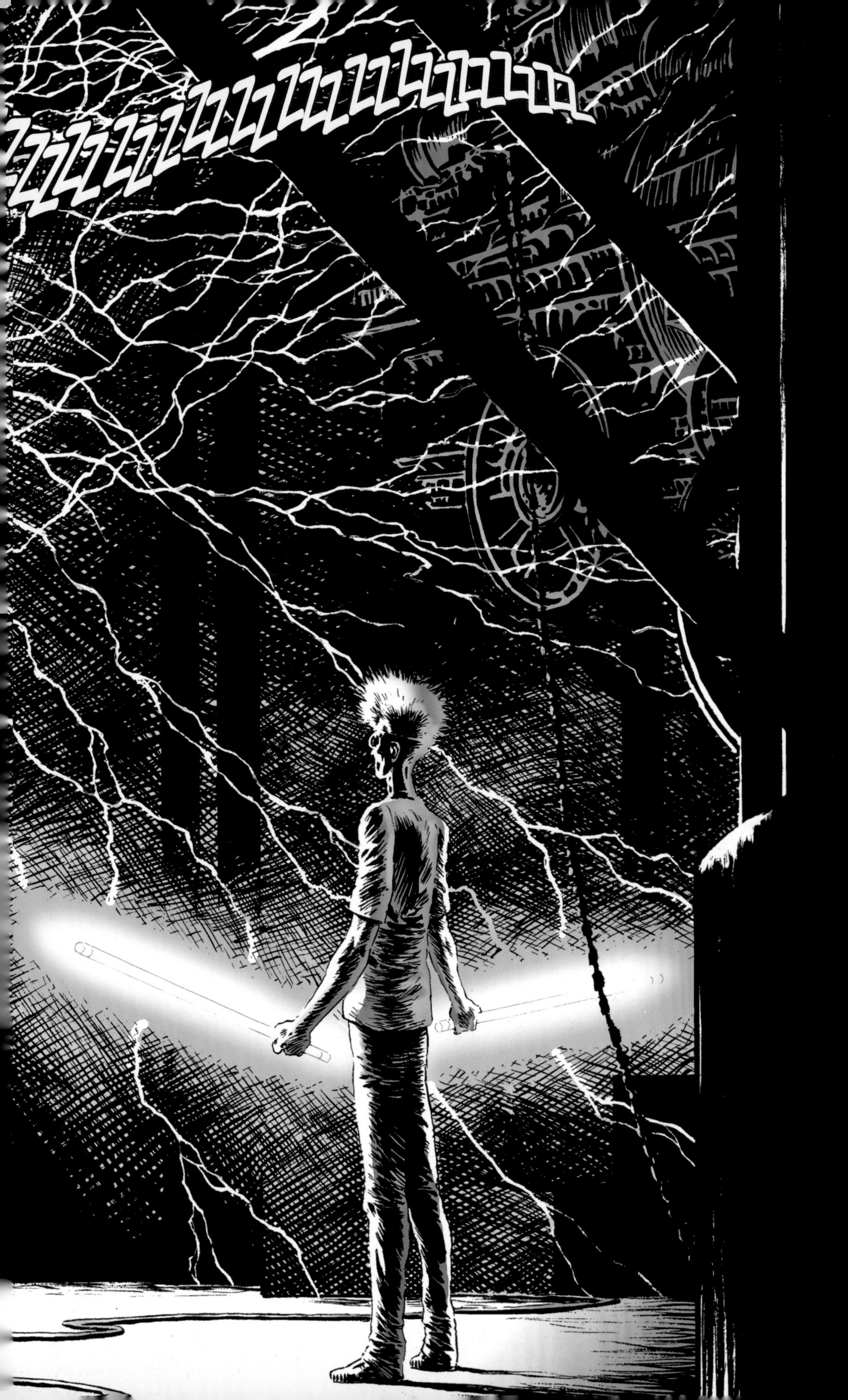

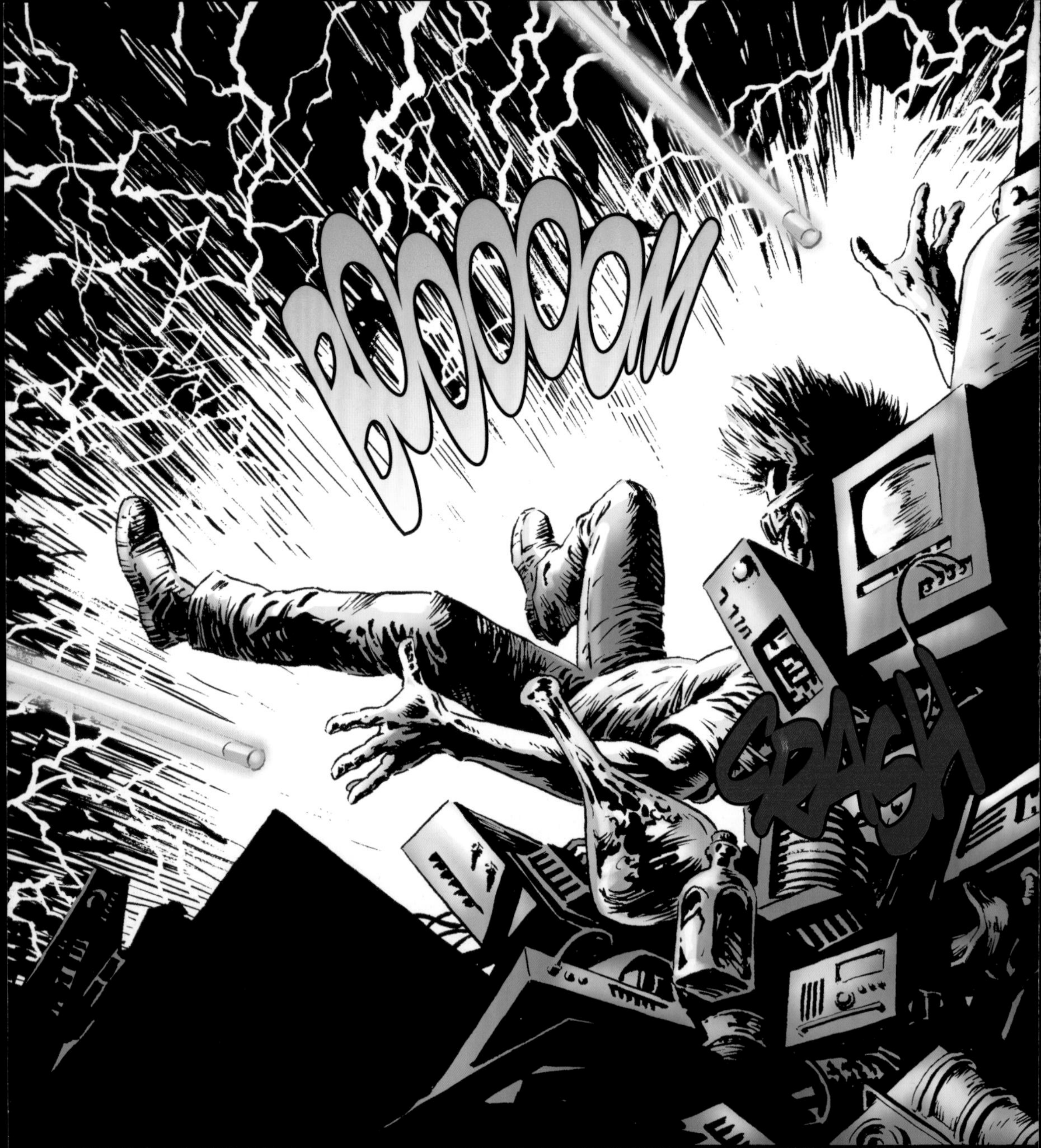
BOOOOOM
CRASH

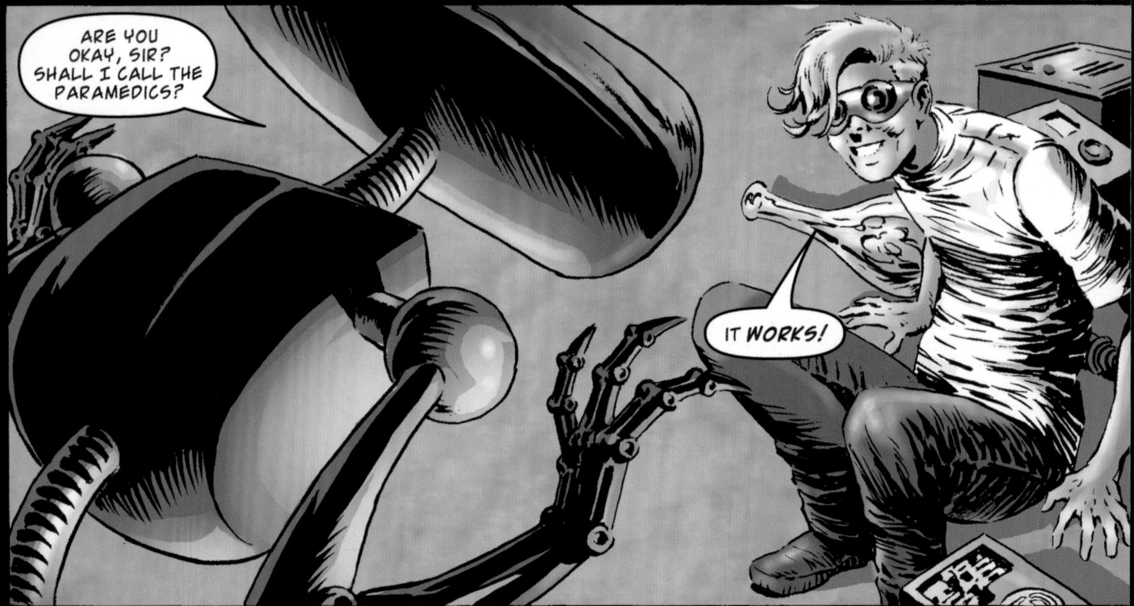
ARE YOU OKAY, SIR? SHALL I CALL THE PARAMEDICS?
IT WORKS!

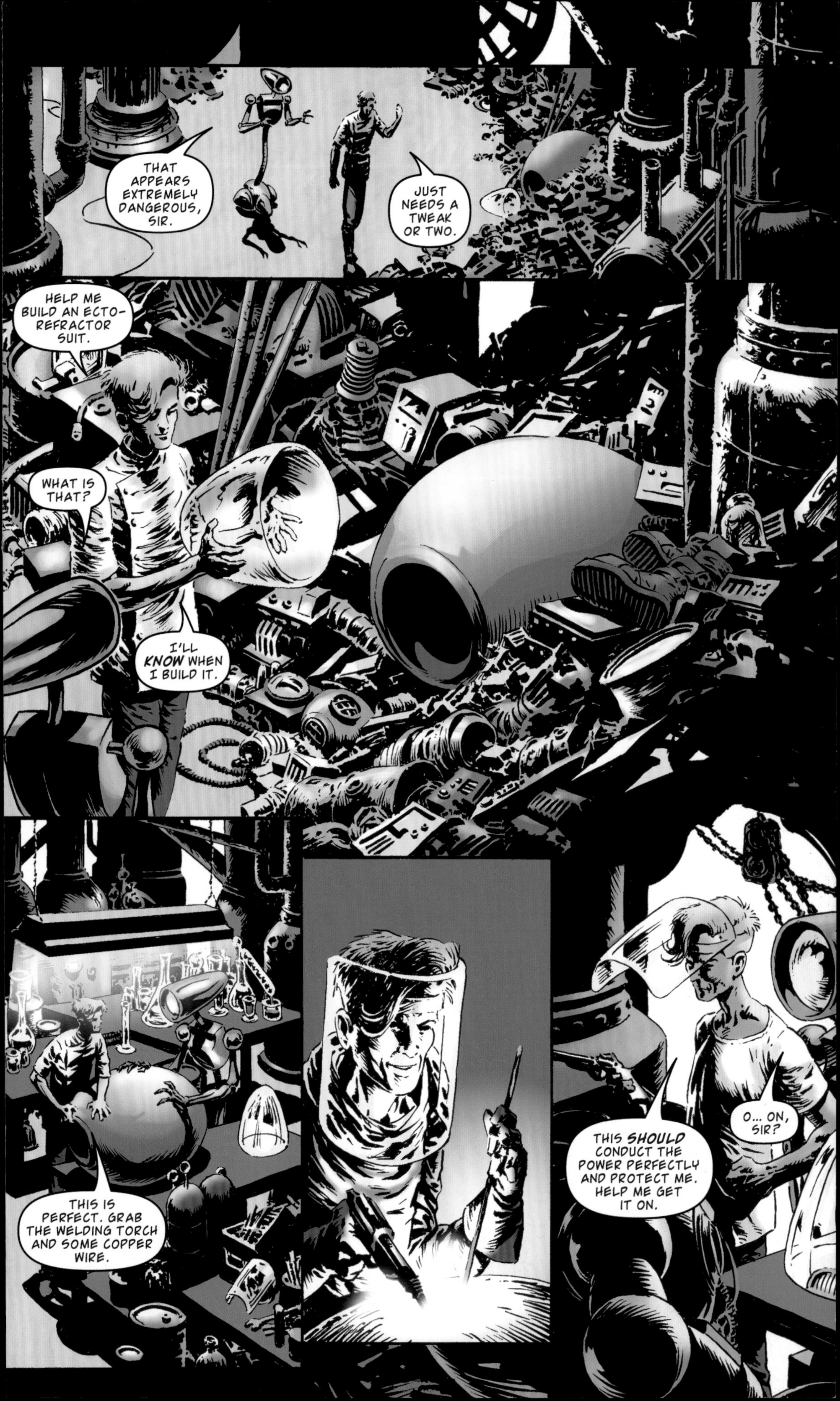
THAT APPEARS EXTREMELY DANGEROUS, SIR.
JUST NEEDS A TWEAK OR TWO.
HELP ME BUILD AN ECTO-REFRACTOR SUIT.
WHAT IS THAT?
I'LL KNOW WHEN I BUILD IT.
THIS IS PERFECT. GRAB THE WELDING TORCH AND SOME COPPER WIRE.
THIS SHOULD CONDUCT THE POWER PERFECTLY AND PROTECT ME. HELP ME GET IT ON.
O... ON, SIR?

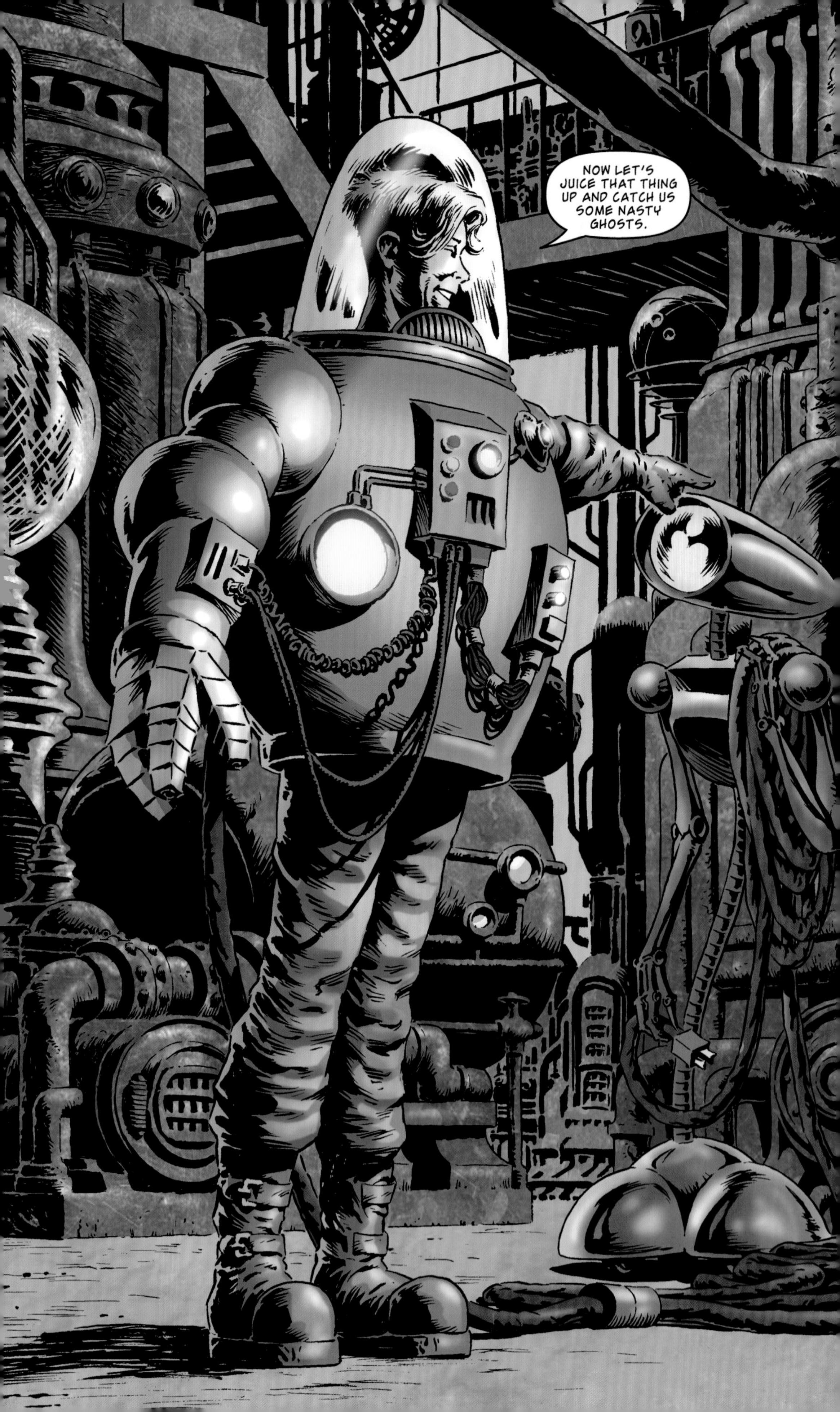
NOW LET'S JUICE THAT THING UP AND CATCH US SOME NASTY GHOSTS.

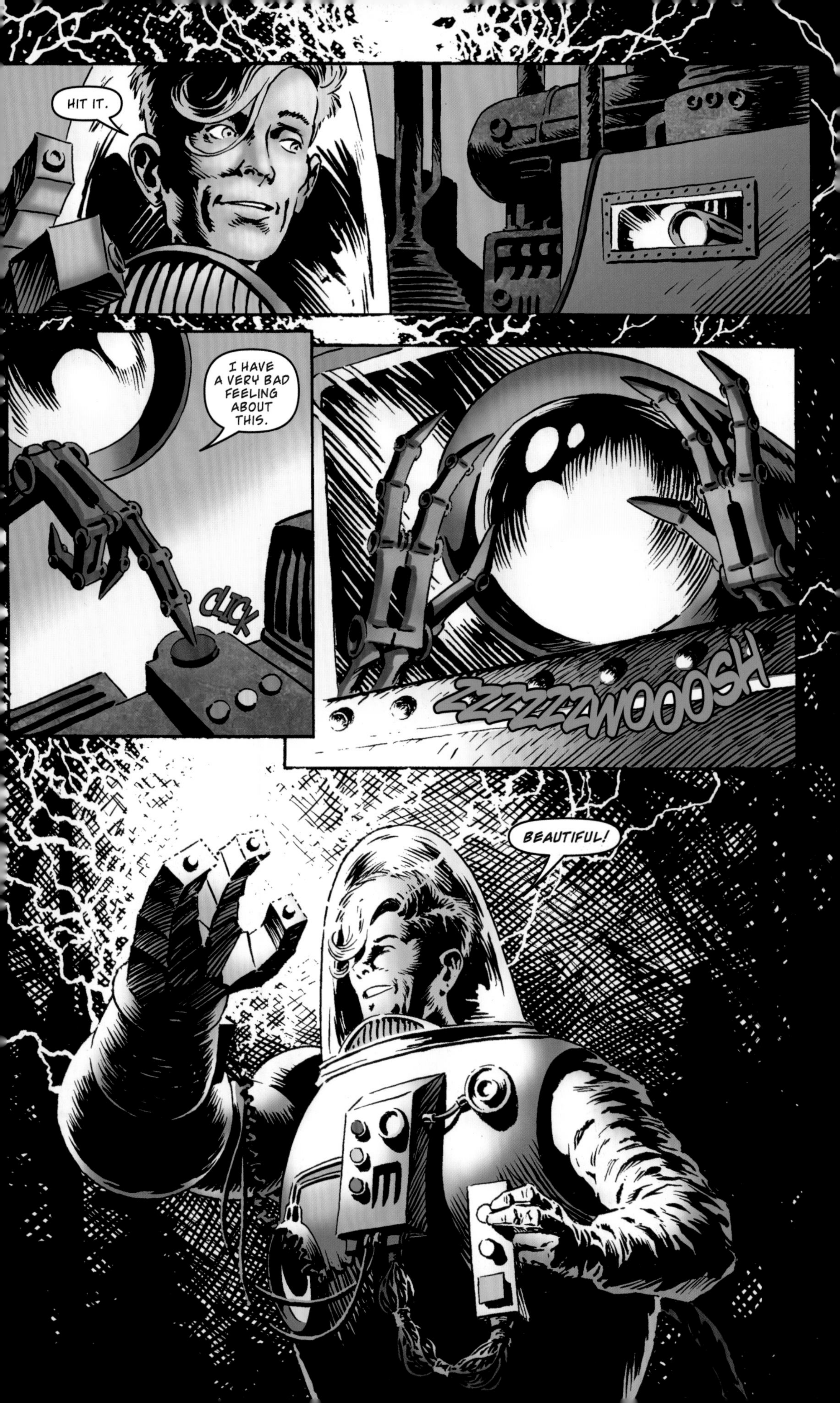
HIT IT.
I HAVE A VERY BAD FEELING ABOUT THIS.
CLICK
ZZZZZZWOOOOSH
BEAUTIFUL!

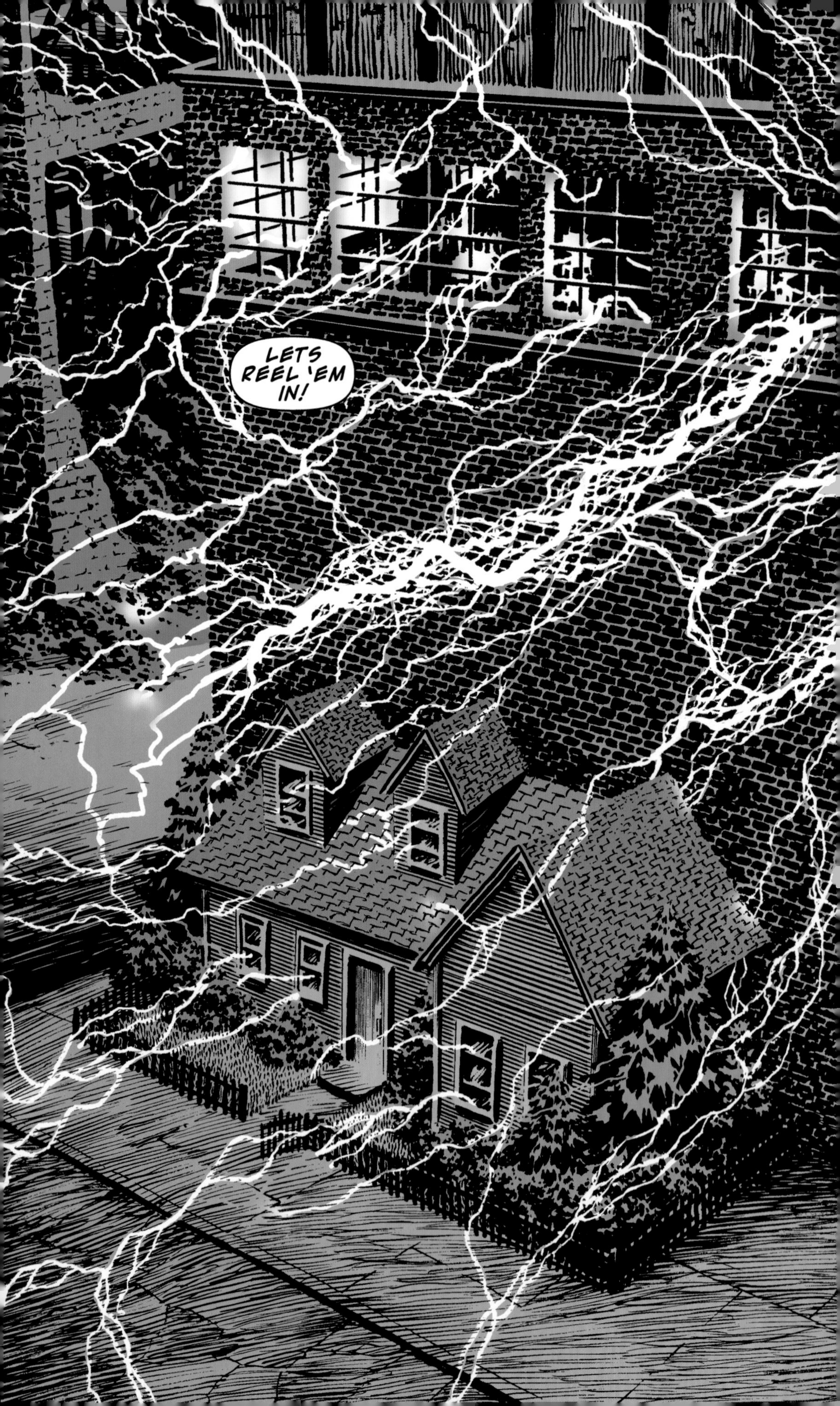
LETS REEL 'EM IN!

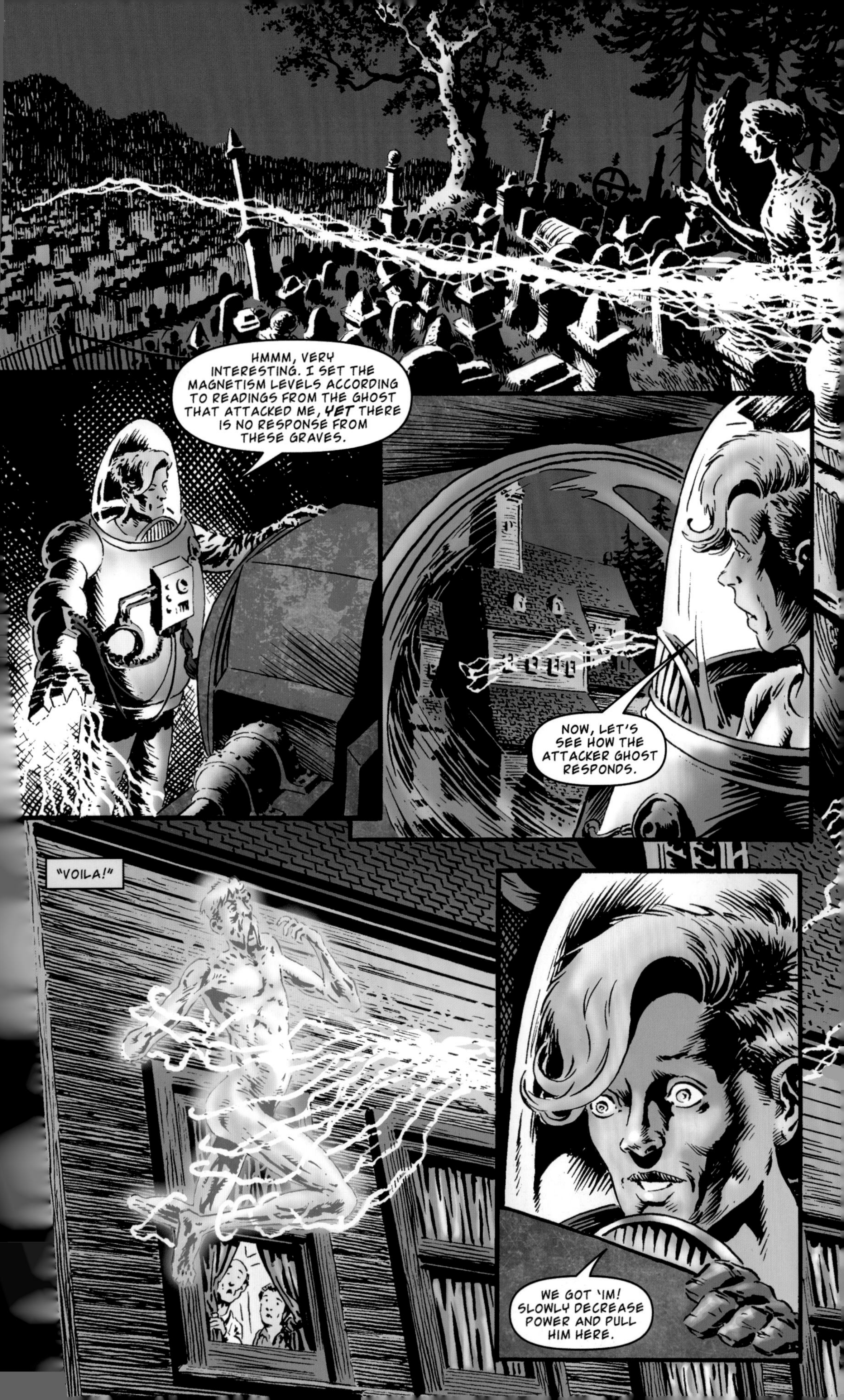
HMMM, VERY INTERESTING. I SET THE MAGNETISM LEVELS ACCORDING TO READINGS FROM THE GHOST THAT ATTACKED ME, YET THERE IS NO RESPONSE FROM THESE GRAVES.
NOW, LET'S SEE HOW THE ATTACKER GHOST RESPONDS.
"VOILA!"
WE GOT 'IM! SLOWLY DECREASE POWER AND PULL HIM HERE.

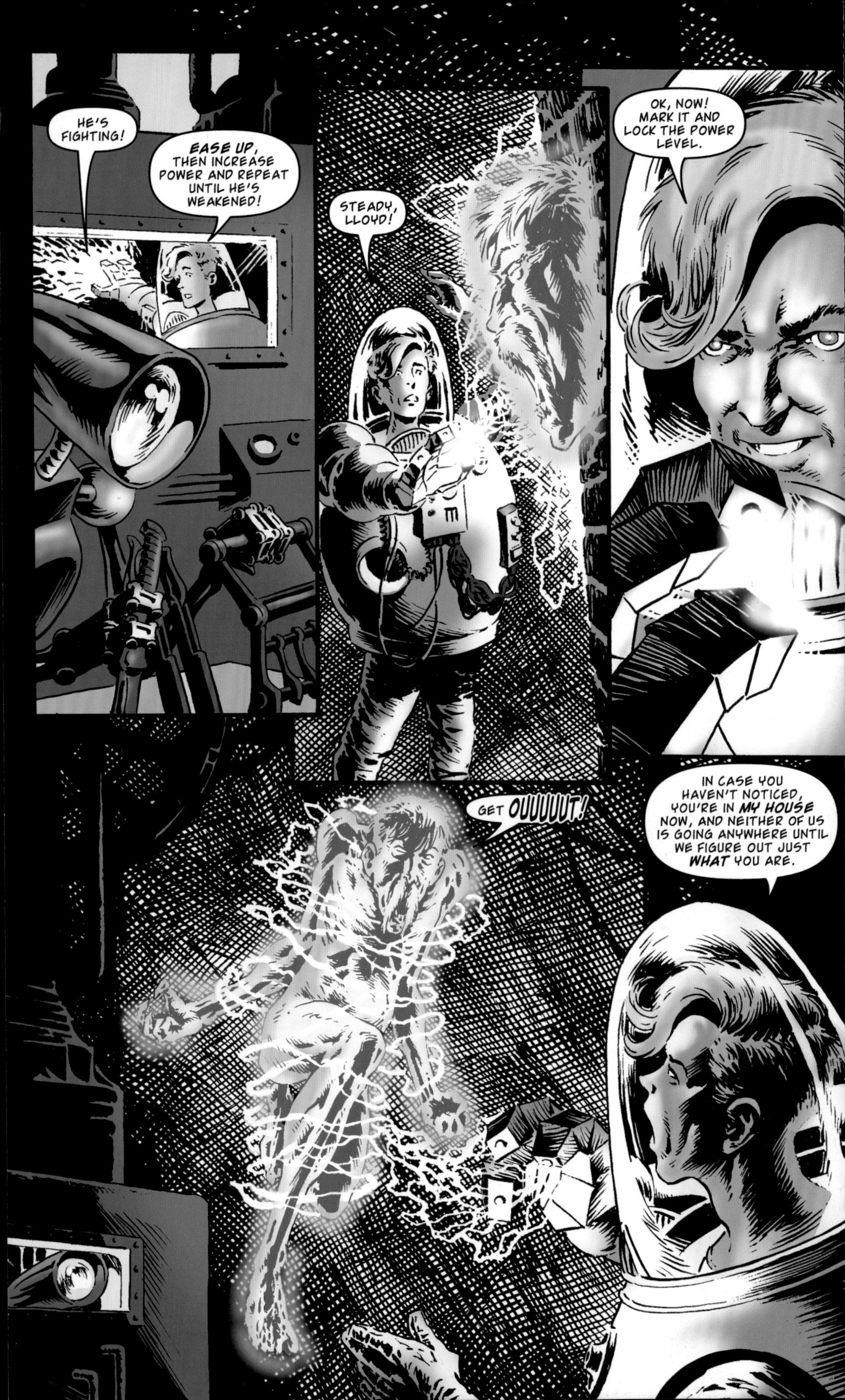
HE'S FIGHTING!
EASE UP, THEN INCREASE POWER AND REPEAT UNTIL HE'S WEAKENED!
STEADY, LLOYD!
OK, NOW! MARK IT AND LOCK THE POWER LEVEL.
GET OUUUUUT!
IN CASE YOU HAVEN'T NOTICED, YOU'RE IN MY HOUSE NOW, AND NEITHER OF US IS GOING ANYWHERE UNTIL WE FIGURE OUT JUST WHAT YOU ARE.

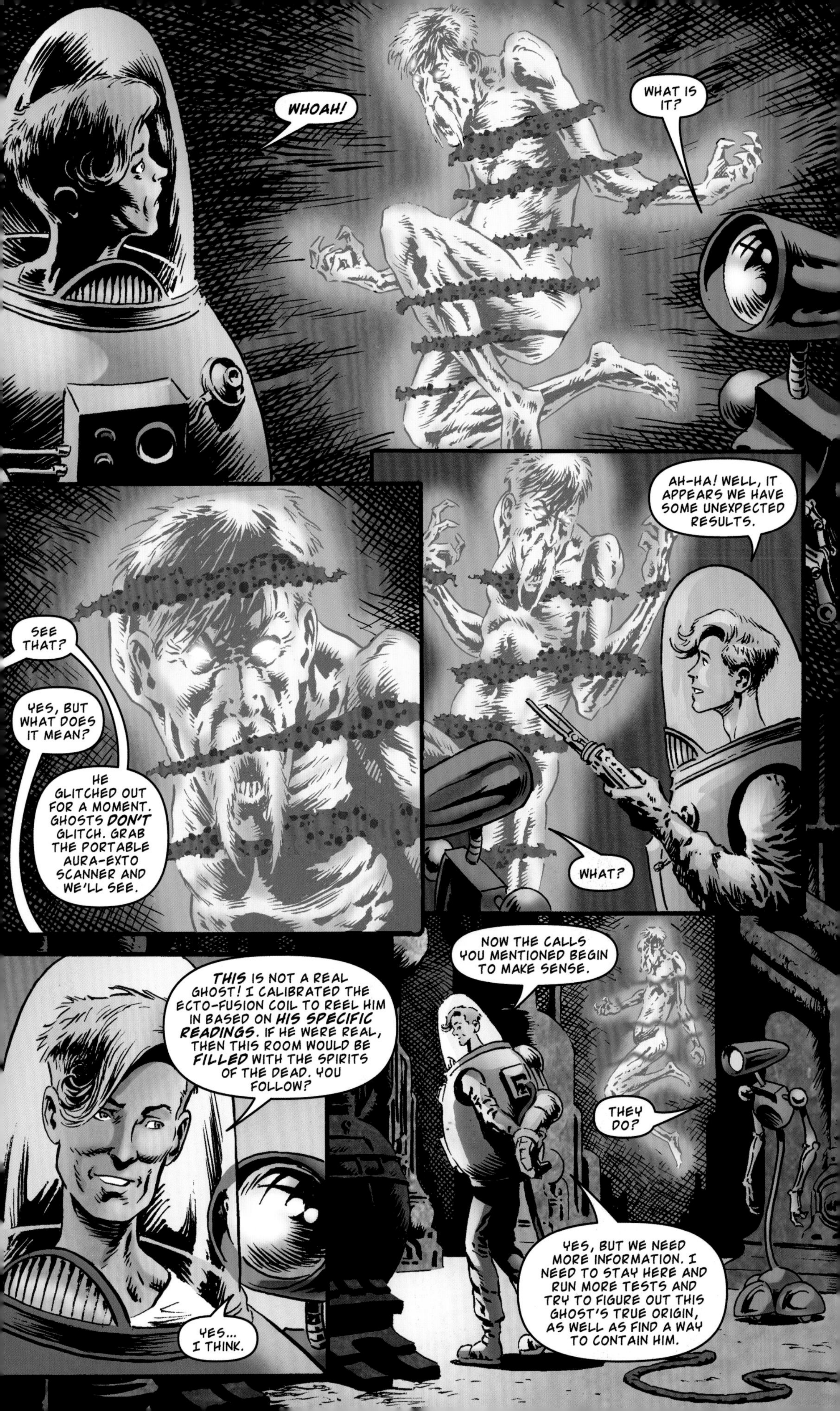
WHOAH!
WHAT IS IT?
AH-HA! WELL, IT APPEARS WE HAVE SOME UNEXPECTED RESULTS.
WHAT?
SEE THAT?
YES, BUT WHAT DOES IT MEAN?
HE GLITCHED OUT FOR A MOMENT. GHOSTS DON'T GLITCH. GRAB THE PORTABLE AURA-EXTO SCANNER AND WE'LL SEE.
THIS IS NOT A REAL GHOST! I CALIBRATED THE ECTO-FUSION COIL TO REEL HIM IN BASED ON HIS SPECIFIC READINGS. IF HE WERE REAL, THEN THIS ROOM WOULD BE FILLED WITH THE SPIRITS OF THE DEAD. YOU FOLLOW?
YES... I THINK.
NOW THE CALLS YOU MENTIONED BEGIN TO MAKE SENSE.
THEY DO?
YES, BUT WE NEED MORE INFORMATION. I NEED TO STAY HERE AND RUN MORE TESTS AND TRY TO FIGURE OUT THIS GHOST'S TRUE ORIGIN, AS WELL AS FIND A WAY TO CONTAIN HIM.

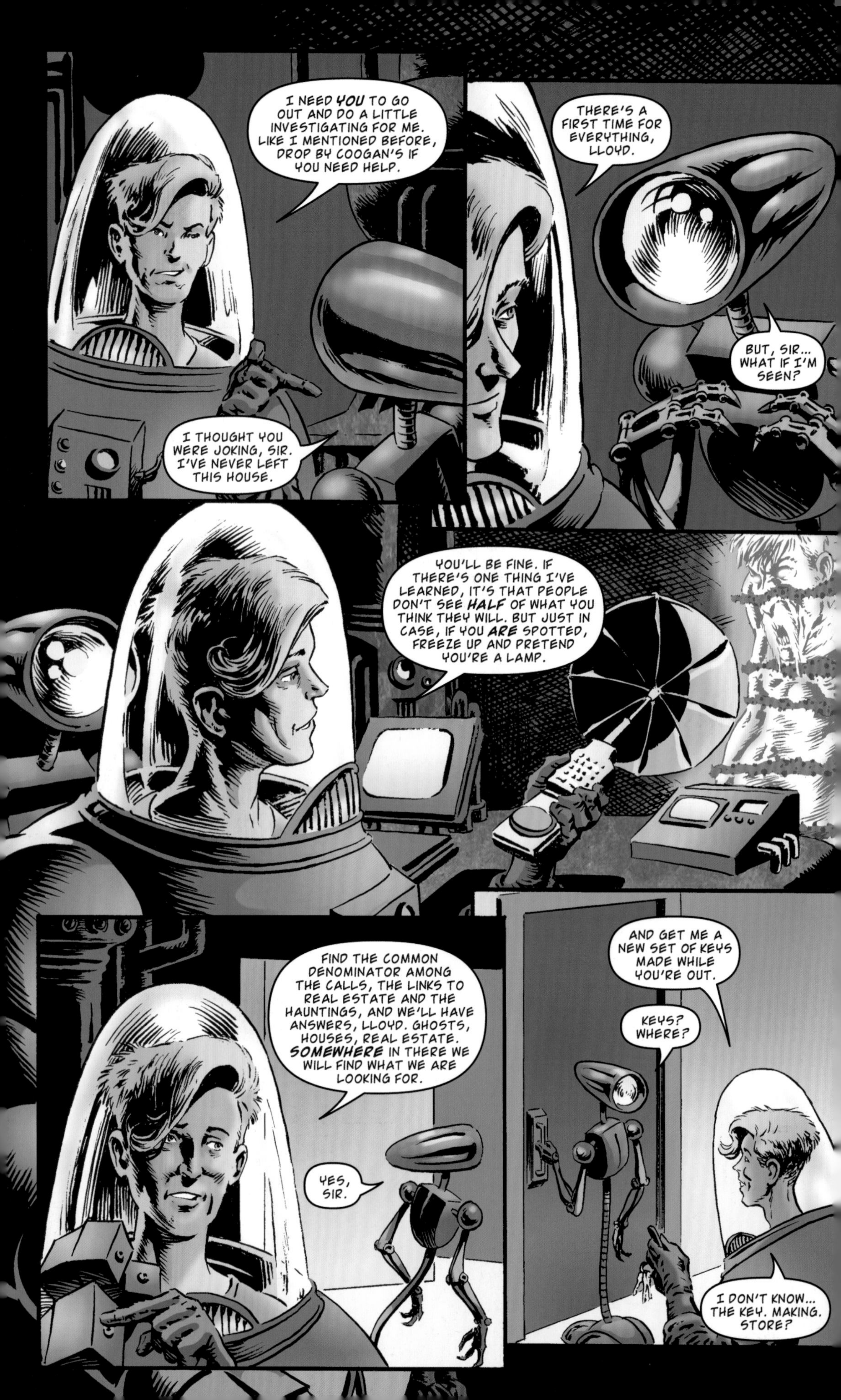
I NEED **YOU** TO GO OUT AND DO A LITTLE INVESTIGATING FOR ME. LIKE I MENTIONED BEFORE, DROP BY COOGAN'S IF YOU NEED HELP.
I THOUGHT YOU WERE JOKING, SIR. I'VE NEVER LEFT THIS HOUSE.
THERE'S A FIRST TIME FOR EVERYTHING, LLOYD.
BUT, SIR... WHAT IF I'M SEEN?
YOU'LL BE FINE. IF THERE'S ONE THING I'VE LEARNED, IT'S THAT PEOPLE DON'T SEE **HALF** OF WHAT YOU THINK THEY WILL. BUT JUST IN CASE, IF YOU **ARE** SPOTTED, FREEZE UP AND PRETEND YOU'RE A LAMP.
FIND THE COMMON DENOMINATOR AMONG THE CALLS, THE LINKS TO REAL ESTATE AND THE HAUNTINGS, AND WE'LL HAVE ANSWERS, LLOYD. GHOSTS, HOUSES, REAL ESTATE. **SOMEWHERE** IN THERE WE WILL FIND WHAT WE ARE LOOKING FOR.
YES, SIR.
AND GET ME A NEW SET OF KEYS MADE WHILE YOU'RE OUT.
KEYS? WHERE?
I DON'T KNOW... THE KEY. MAKING. STORE?

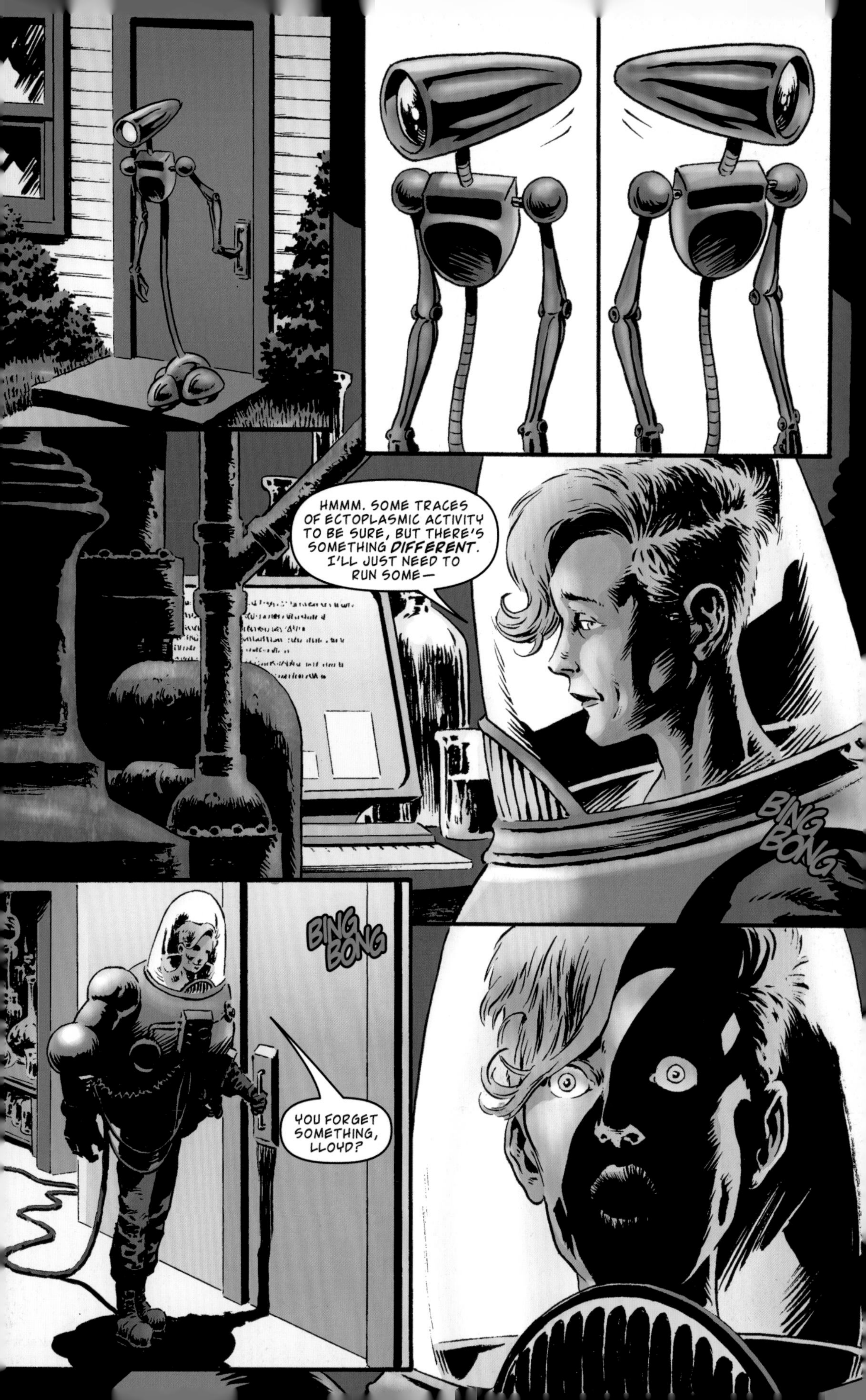
HMMM. SOME TRACES OF ECTOPLASMIC ACTIVITY TO BE SURE, BUT THERE'S SOMETHING *DIFFERENT*. I'LL JUST NEED TO RUN SOME—
BING BONG
BING BONG
YOU FORGET SOMETHING, LLOYD?

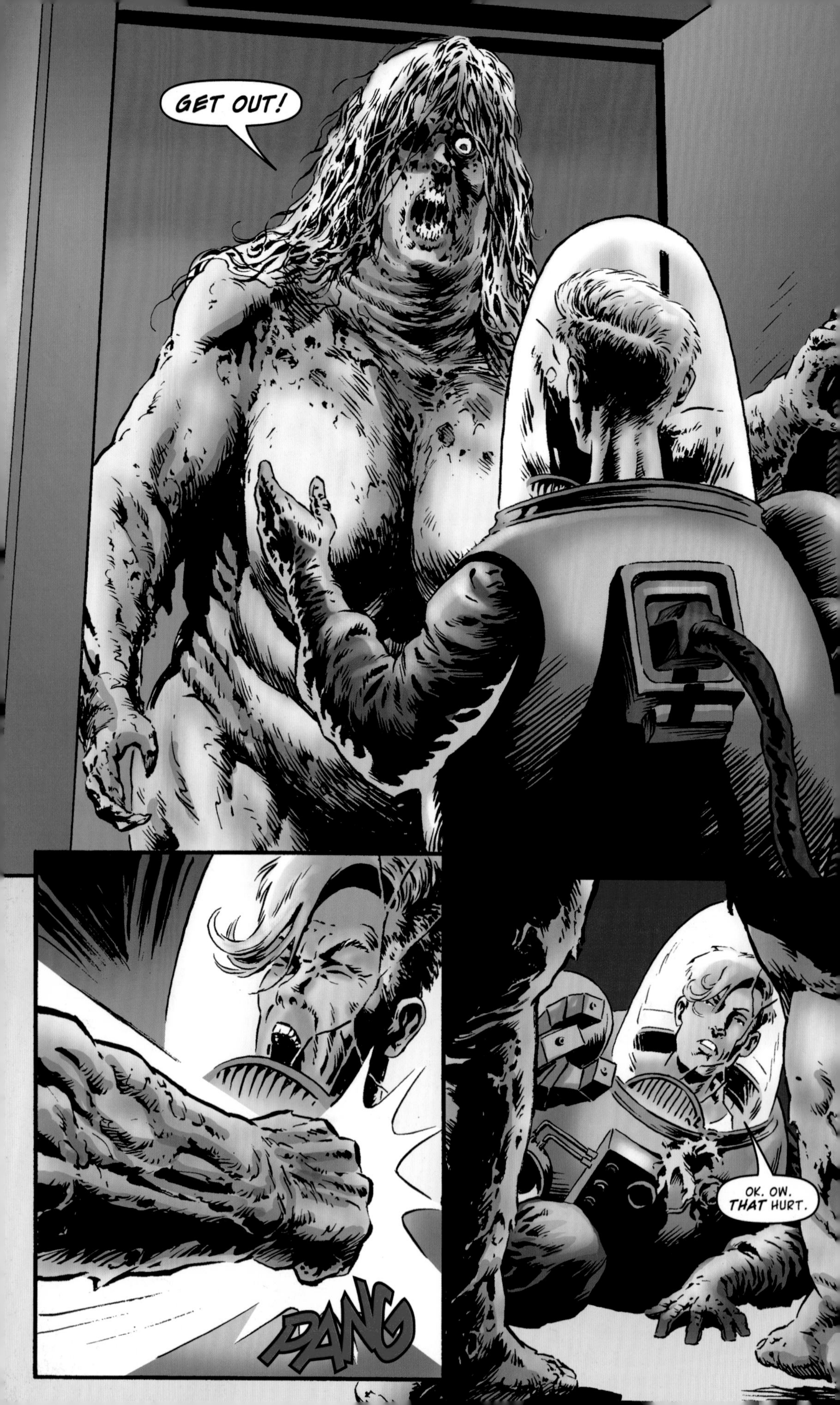
GET OUT!
PANG
OK. OW.
THAT HURT.

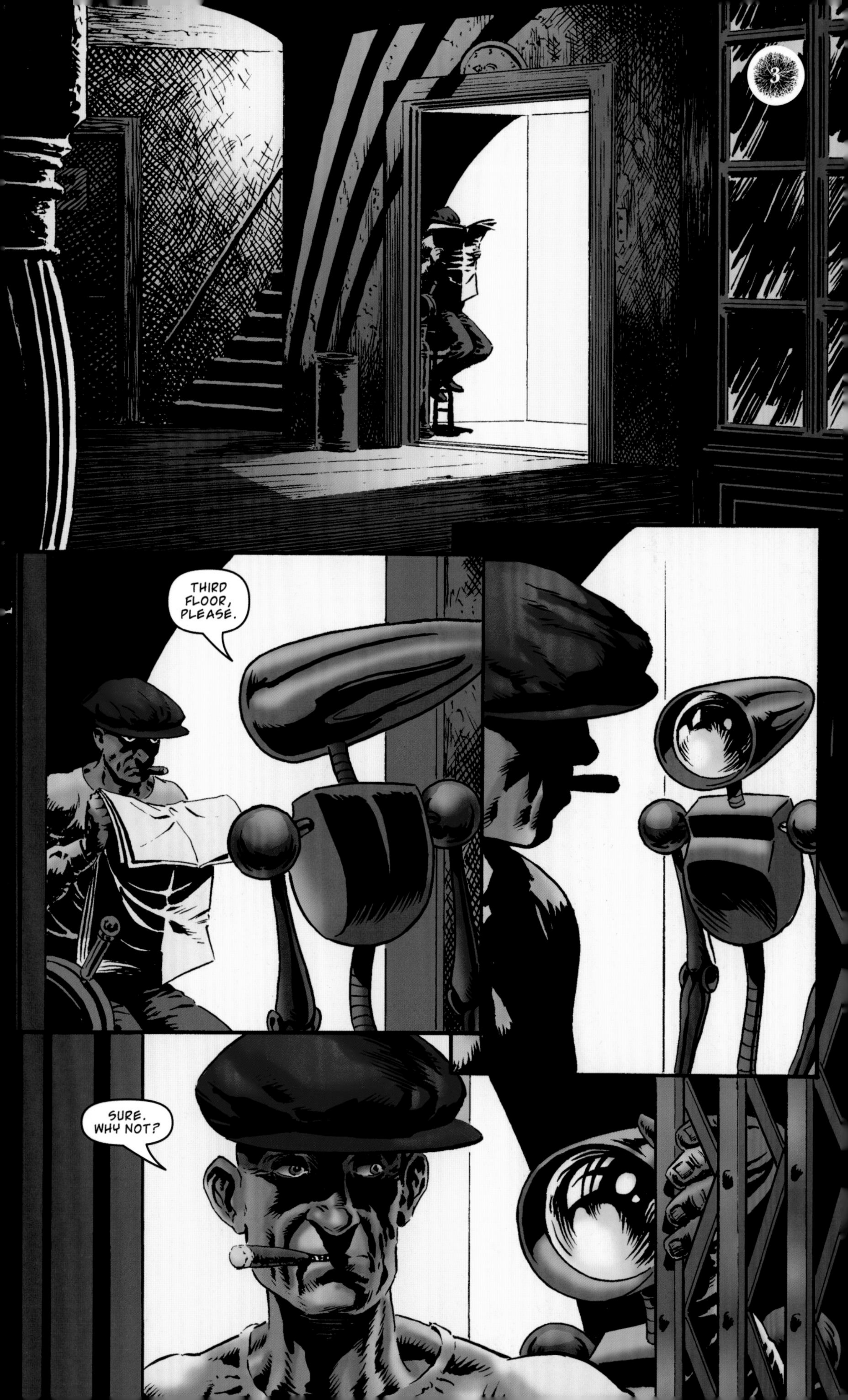
THIRD FLOOR, PLEASE.
SURE. WHY NOT?

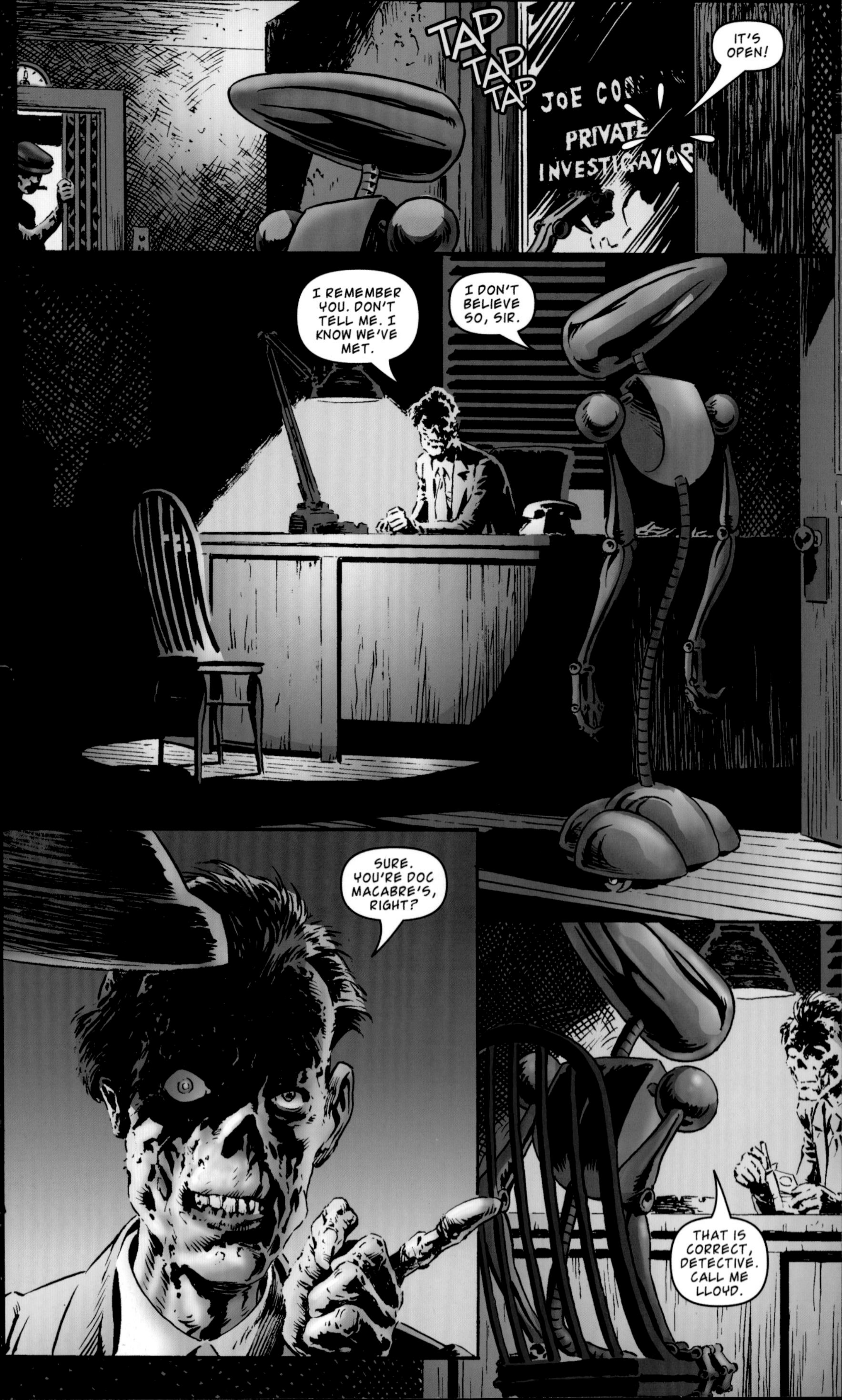
TAP TAP TAP
JOE COB...
PRIVATE
INVESTIGATOR
IT'S OPEN!
I REMEMBER YOU. DON'T TELL ME. I KNOW WE'VE MET.
I DON'T BELIEVE SO, SIR.
SURE. YOU'RE DOC MACABRE'S, RIGHT?
THAT IS CORRECT, DETECTIVE. CALL ME LLOYD.

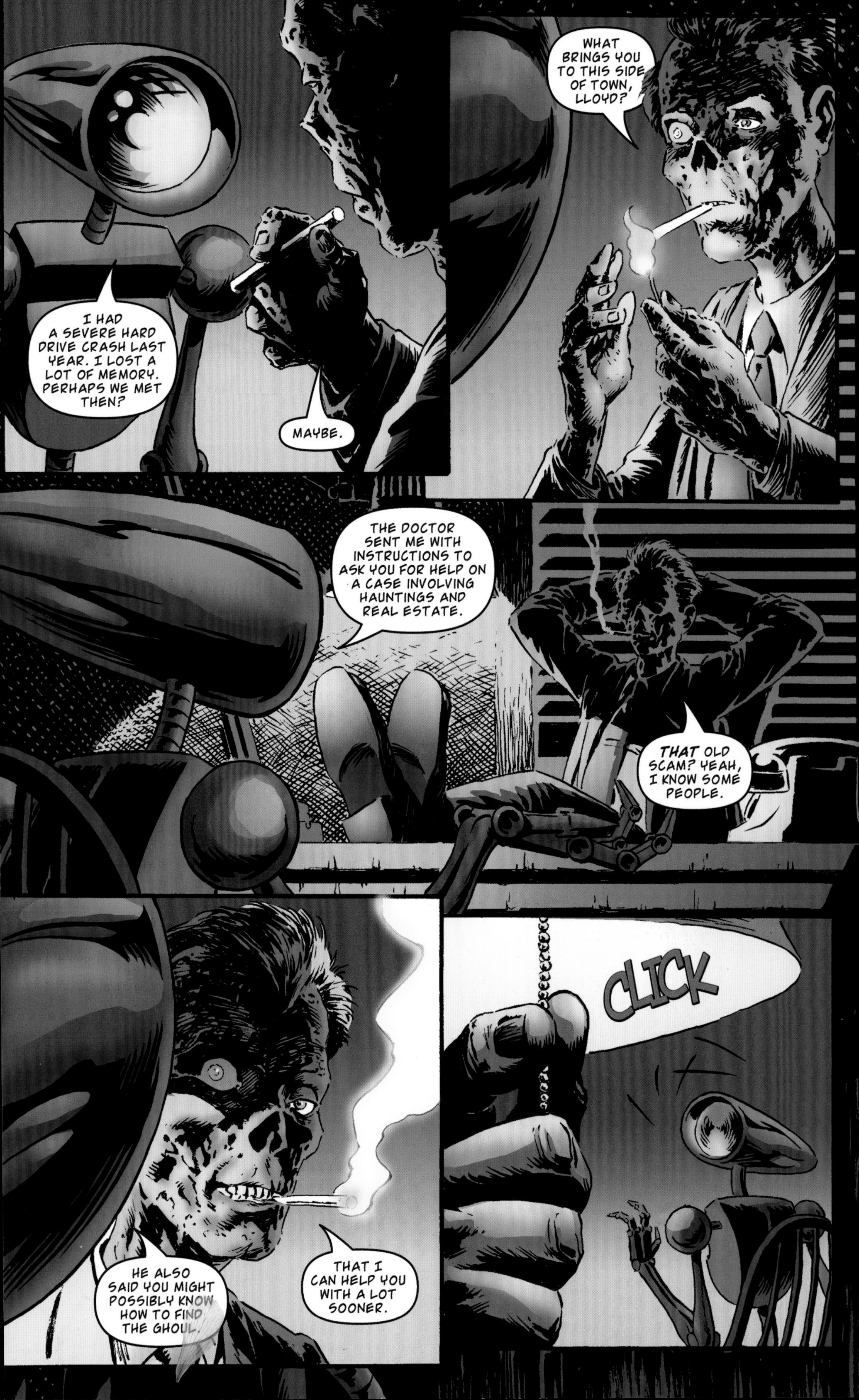
WHAT BRINGS YOU TO THIS SIDE OF TOWN, LLOYD?
I HAD A SEVERE HARD DRIVE CRASH LAST YEAR. I LOST A LOT OF MEMORY. PERHAPS WE MET THEN?
MAYBE.
THE DOCTOR SENT ME WITH INSTRUCTIONS TO ASK YOU FOR HELP ON A CASE INVOLVING HAUNTINGS AND REAL ESTATE.
THAT OLD SCAM? YEAH, I KNOW SOME PEOPLE.
HE ALSO SAID YOU MIGHT POSSIBLY KNOW HOW TO FIND THE GHOUL.
THAT I CAN HELP YOU WITH A LOT SOONER.
CLICK

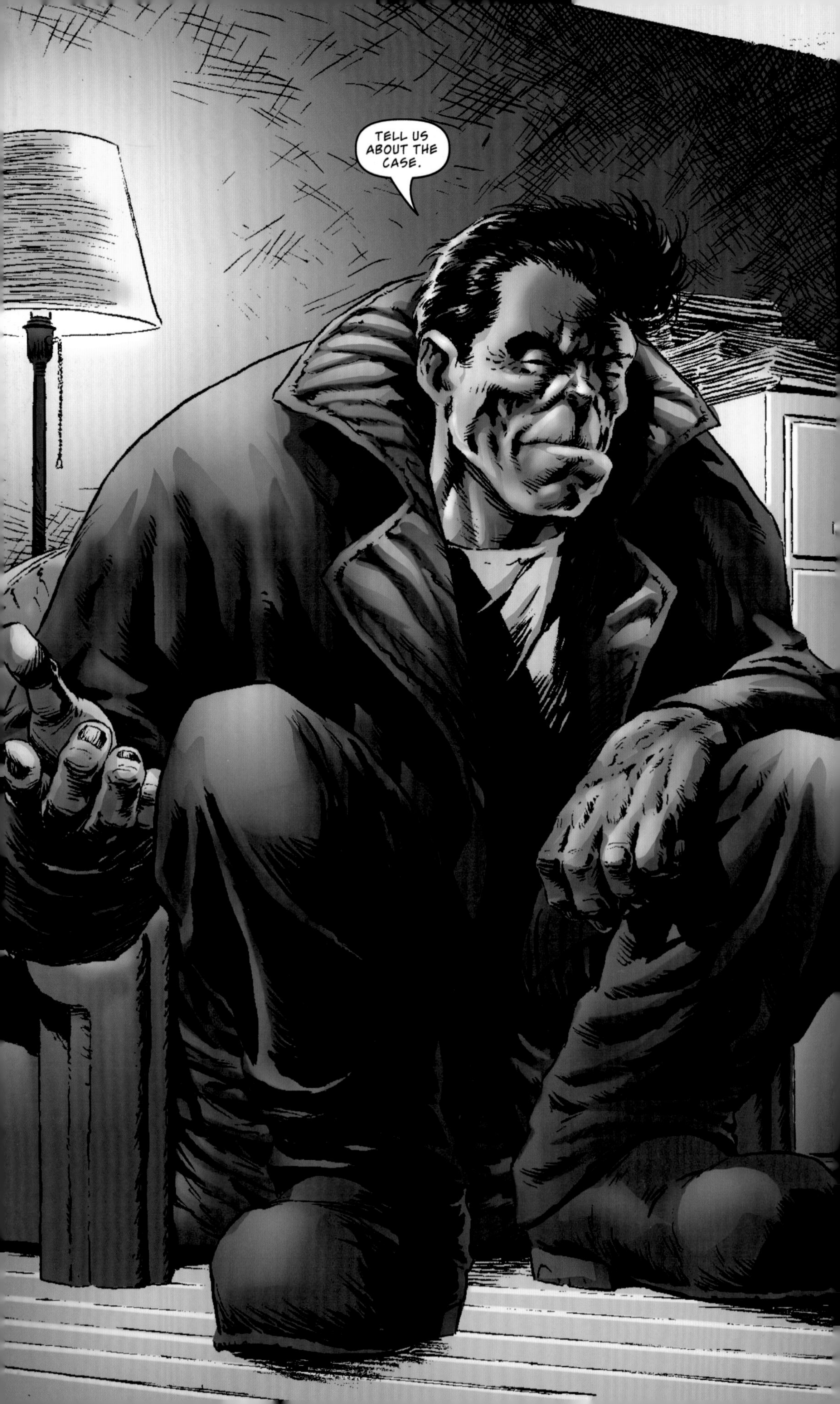
TELL US ABOUT THE CASE.

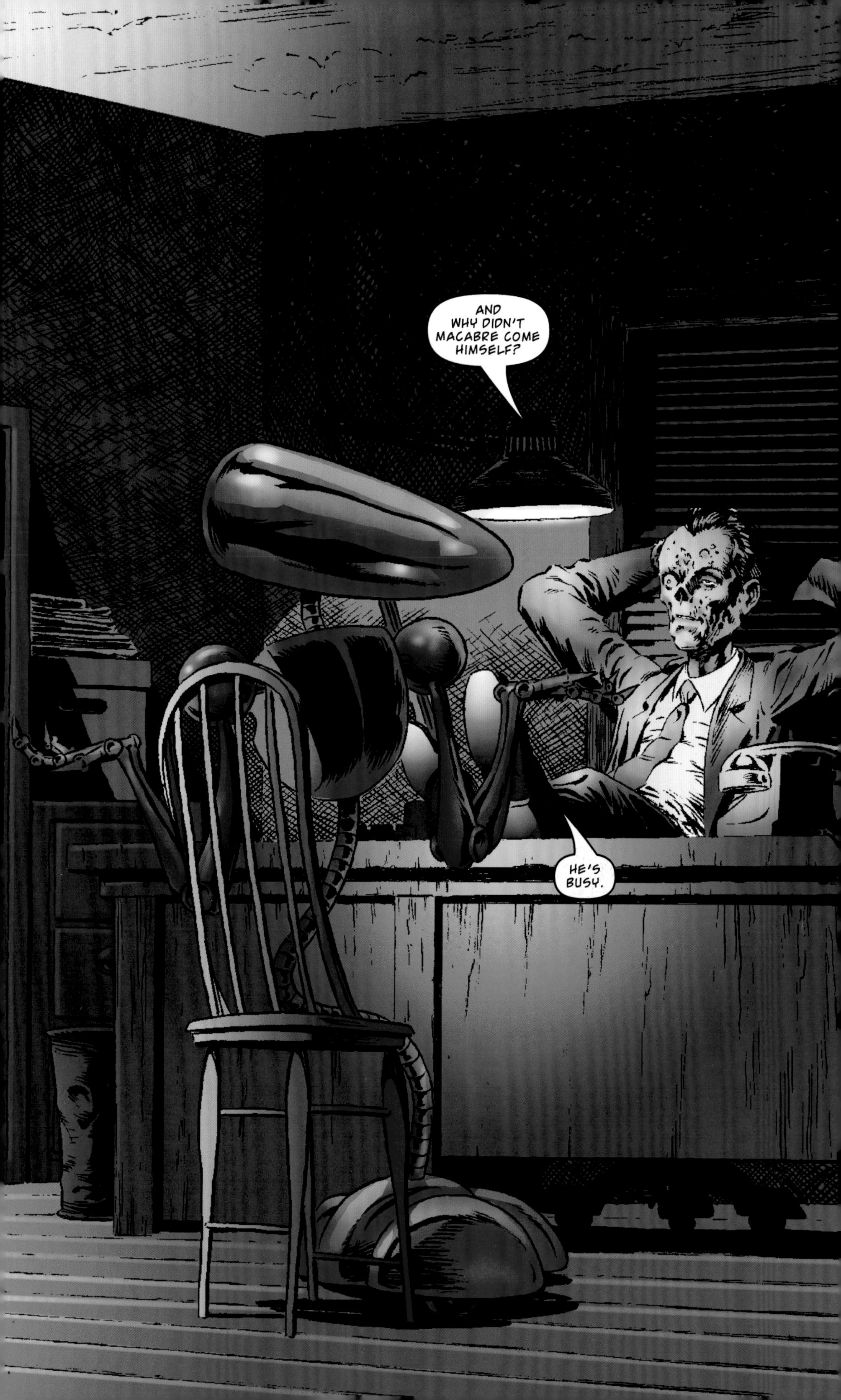
AND WHY DIDN'T MACABRE COME HIMSELF?
HE'S BUSY.

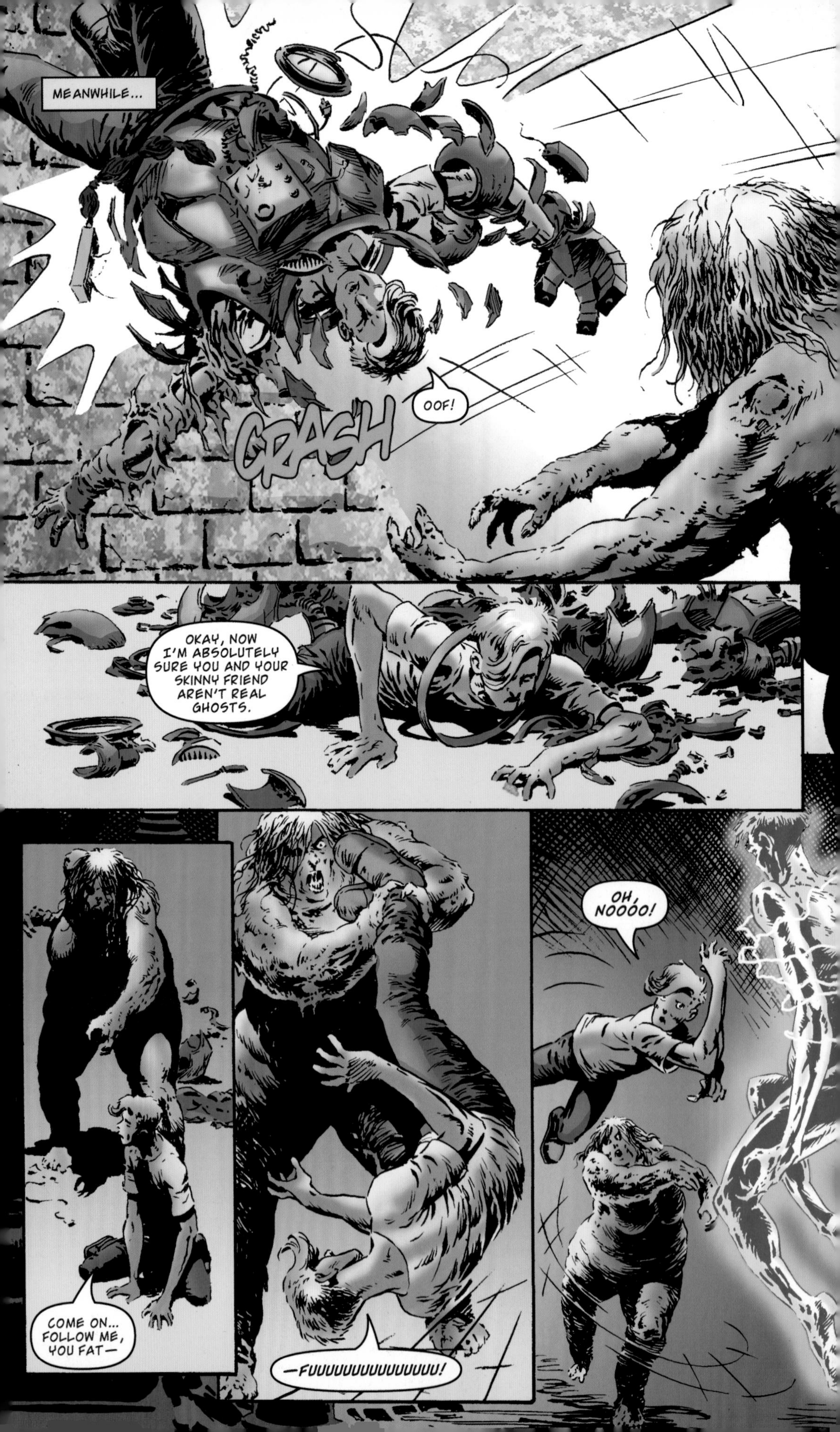
MEANWHILE...
OOF!
CRASH
OKAY, NOW I'M ABSOLUTELY SURE YOU AND YOUR SKINNY FRIEND AREN'T REAL GHOSTS.
COME ON... FOLLOW ME, YOU FAT—
—FUUUUUUUUUUUUUUU!
OH, NOOOO!

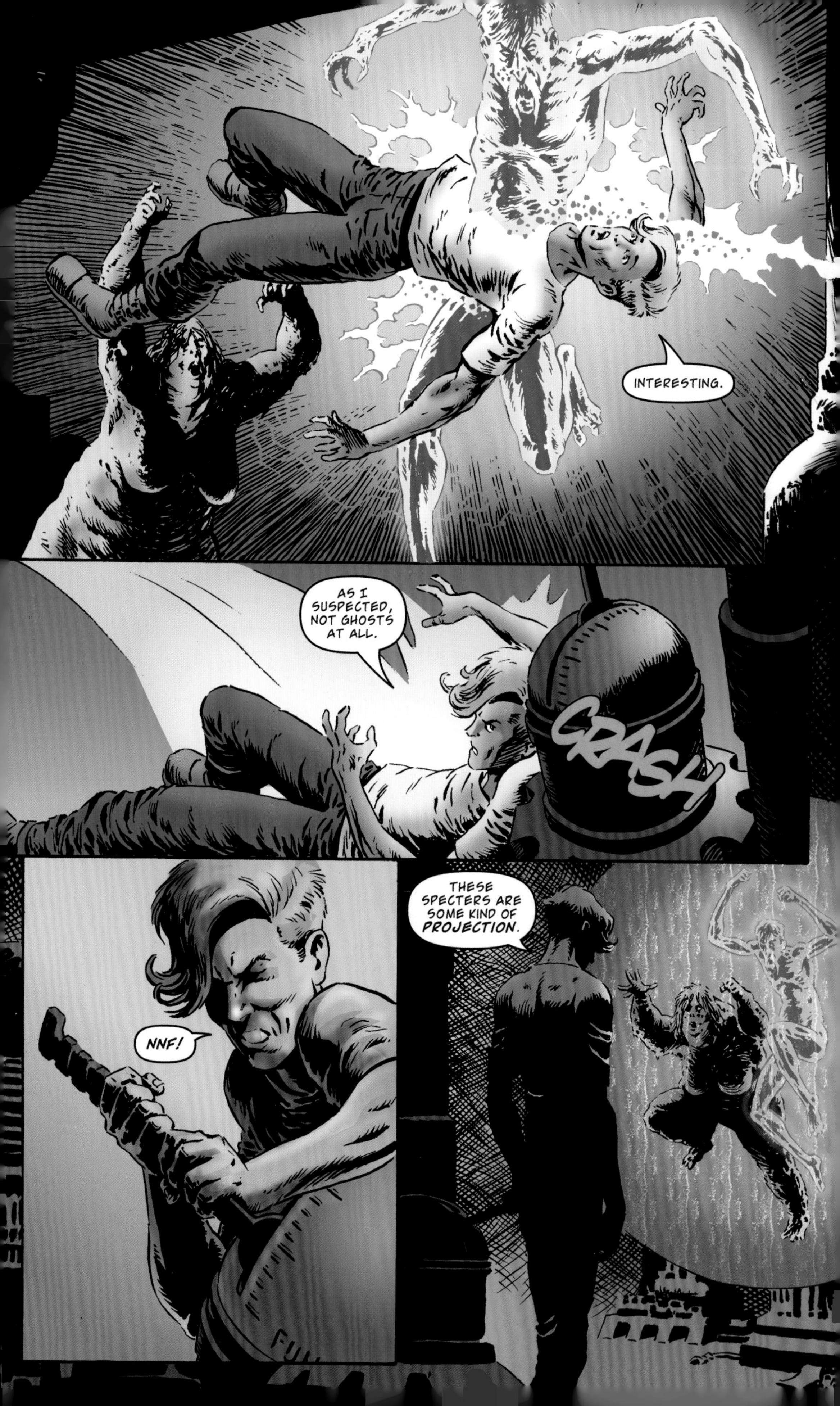
INTERESTING.
AS I SUSPECTED, NOT GHOSTS AT ALL.
CRASH
NNF!
THESE SPECTERS ARE SOME KIND OF PROJECTION.

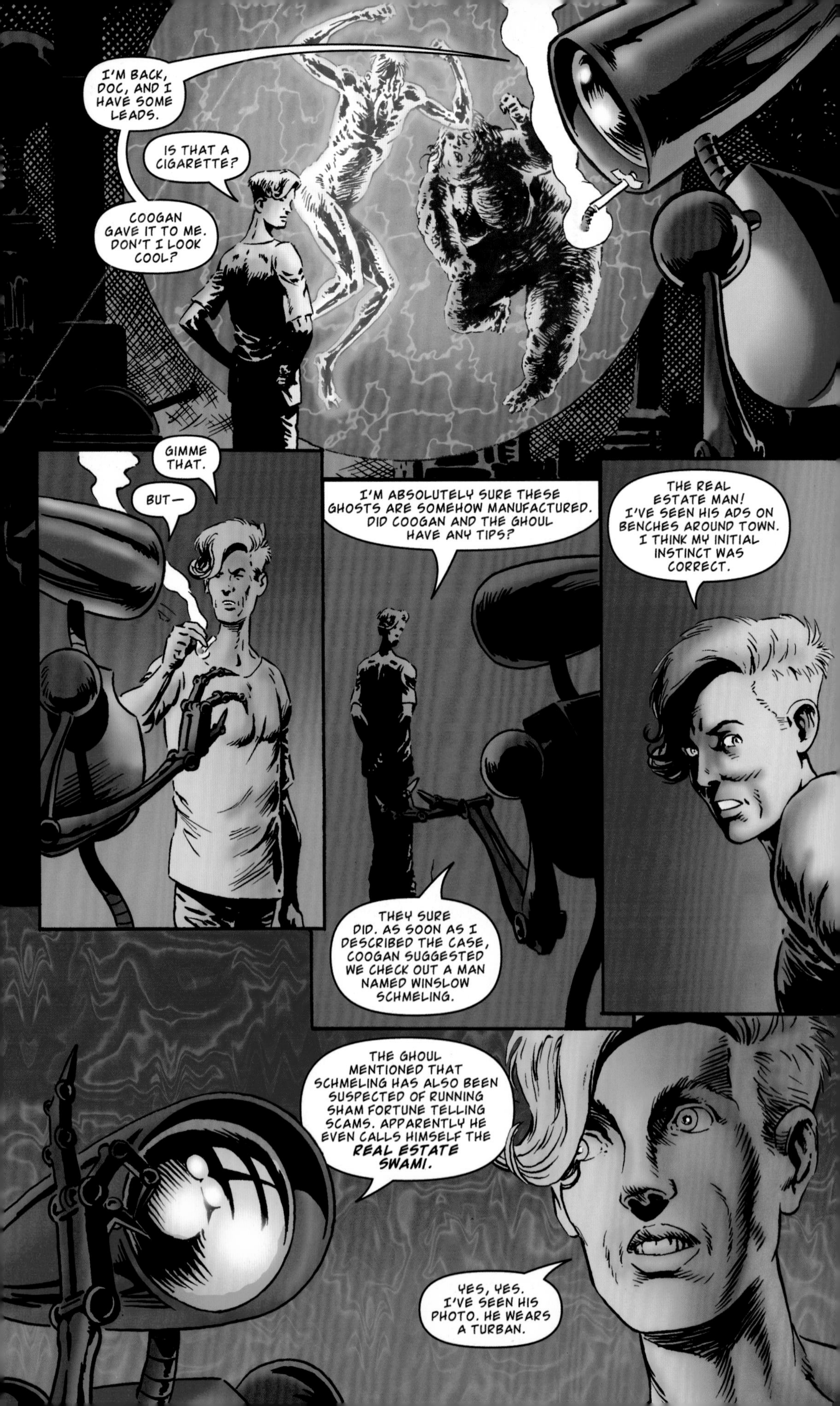

I'M BACK, DOC, AND I HAVE SOME LEADS.
IS THAT A CIGARETTE?
COOGAN GAVE IT TO ME. DON'T I LOOK COOL?
GIMME THAT.
BUT—
I'M ABSOLUTELY SURE THESE GHOSTS ARE SOMEHOW MANUFACTURED. DID COOGAN AND THE GHOUL HAVE ANY TIPS?
THEY SURE DID. AS SOON AS I DESCRIBED THE CASE, COOGAN SUGGESTED WE CHECK OUT A MAN NAMED WINSLOW SCHMELING.
THE REAL ESTATE MAN! I'VE SEEN HIS ADS ON BENCHES AROUND TOWN. I THINK MY INITIAL INSTINCT WAS CORRECT.
THE GHOUL MENTIONED THAT SCHMELING HAS ALSO BEEN SUSPECTED OF RUNNING SHAM FORTUNE TELLING SCAMS. APPARENTLY HE EVEN CALLS HIMSELF THE ***REAL ESTATE SWAMI.***
YES, YES. I'VE SEEN HIS PHOTO. HE WEARS A TURBAN.

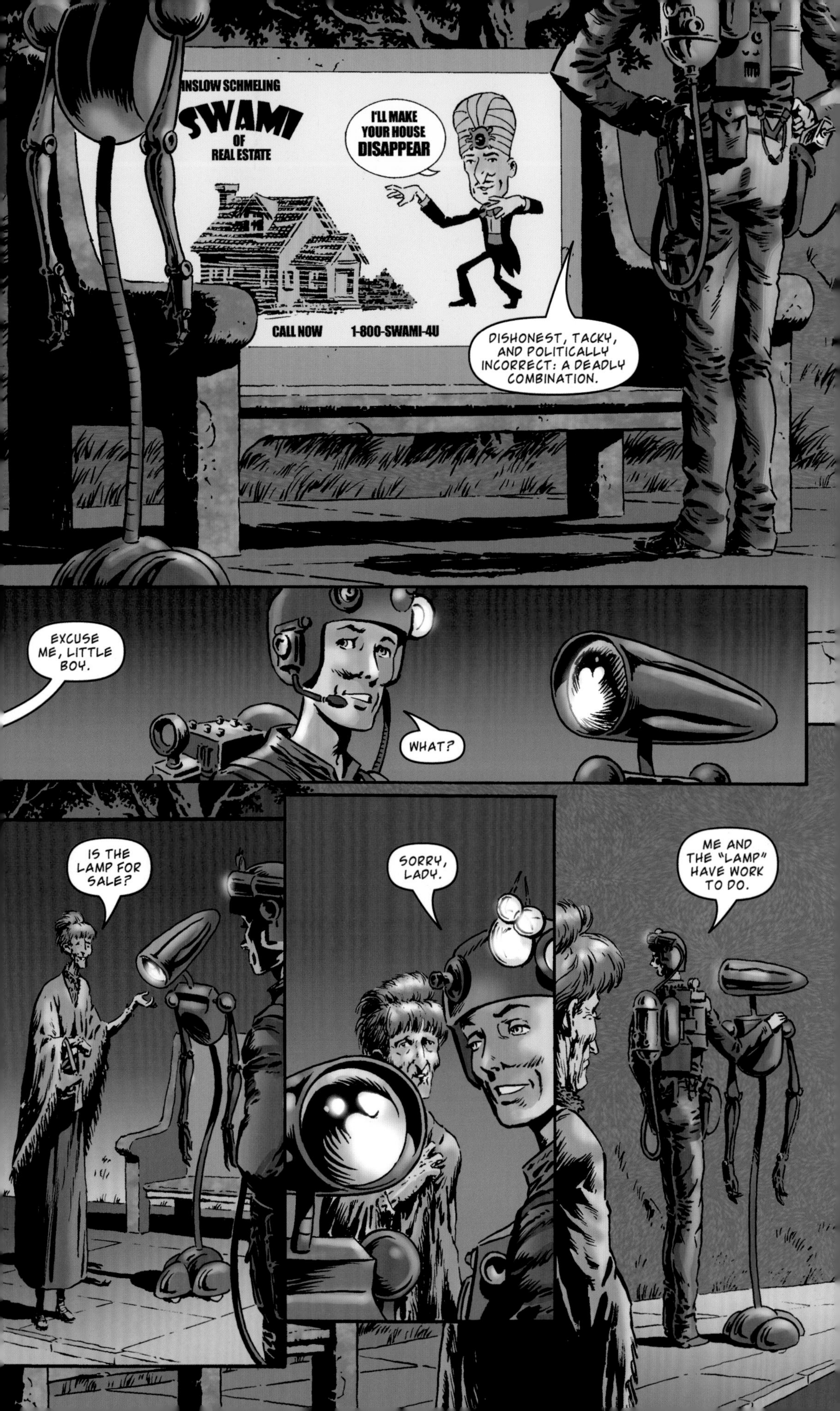
INSLOW SCHMELING
SWAMI
OF
REAL ESTATE
I'LL MAKE YOUR HOUSE DISAPPEAR
CALL NOW 1-800-SWAMI-4U
DISHONEST, TACKY, AND POLITICALLY INCORRECT: A DEADLY COMBINATION.
EXCUSE ME, LITTLE BOY.
WHAT?
IS THE LAMP FOR SALE?
SORRY, LADY.
ME AND THE "LAMP" HAVE WORK TO DO.

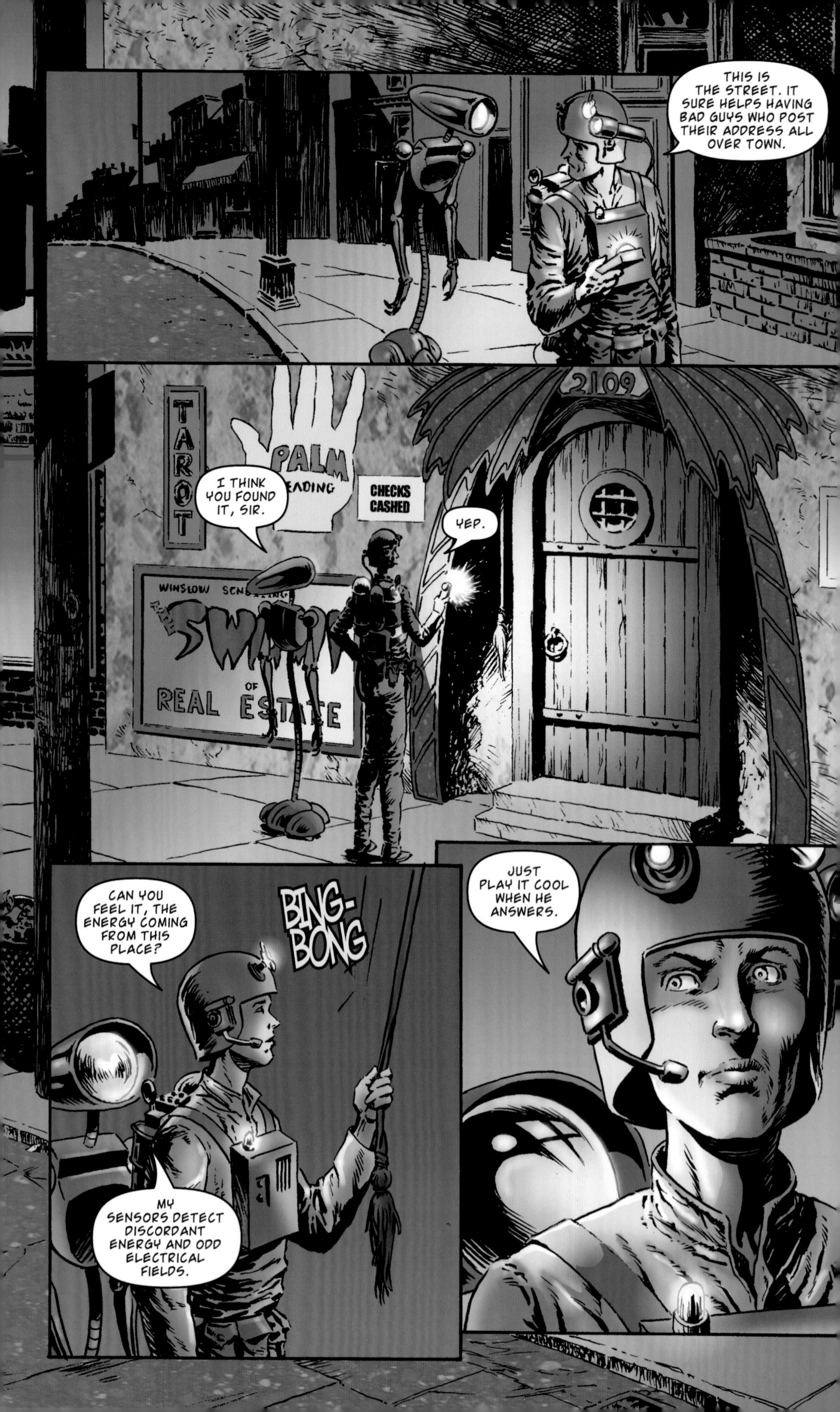
THIS IS THE STREET. IT SURE HELPS HAVING BAD GUYS WHO POST THEIR ADDRESS ALL OVER TOWN.
2109
TAROT
PALM READING
CHECKS CASHED
I THINK YOU FOUND IT, SIR.
YEP.
REAL ESTATE
CAN YOU FEEL IT, THE ENERGY COMING FROM THIS PLACE?
BING-BONG
MY SENSORS DETECT DISCORDANT ENERGY AND ODD ELECTRICAL FIELDS.
JUST PLAY IT COOL WHEN HE ANSWERS.

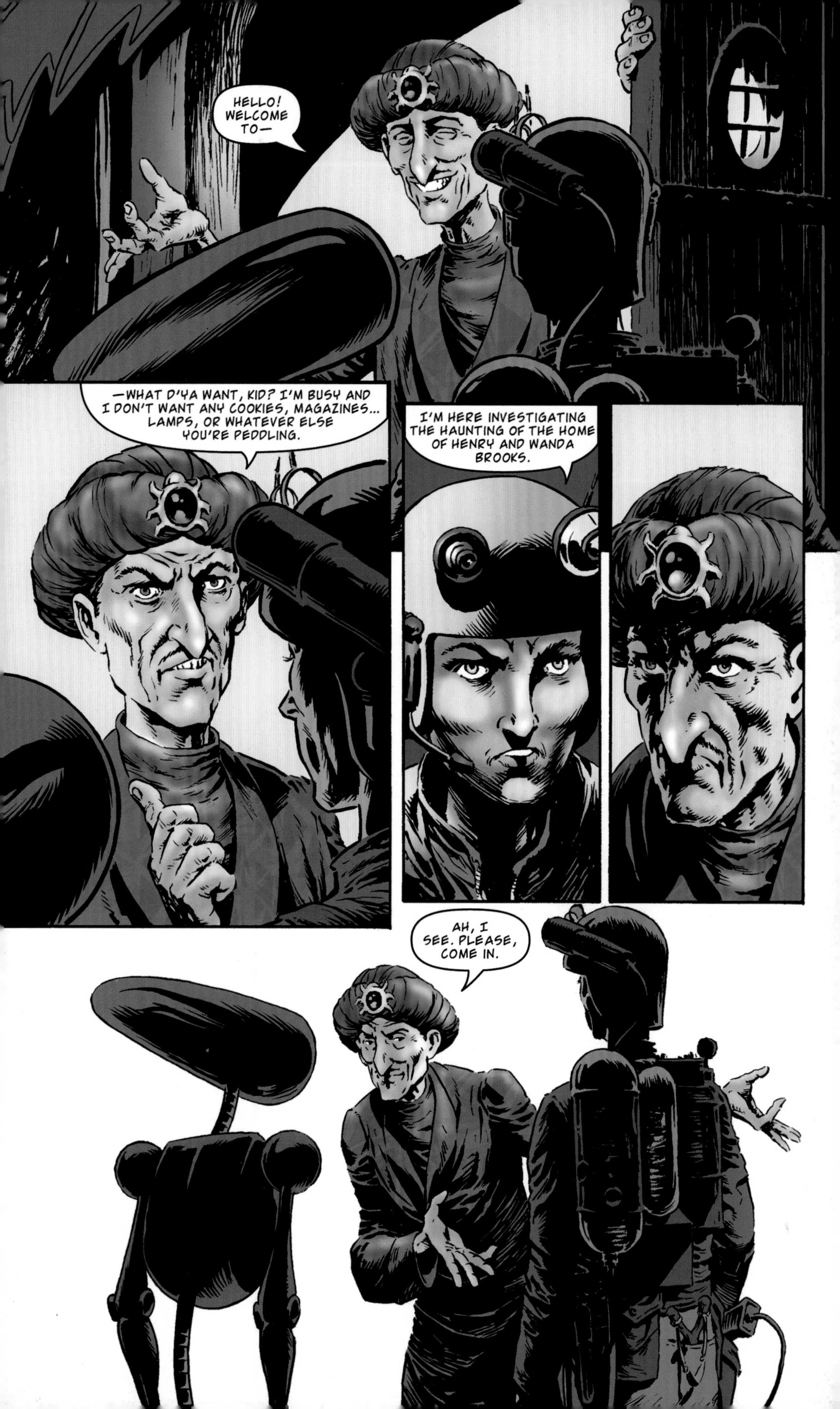
HELLO! WELCOME TO—
—WHAT D'YA WANT, KID? I'M BUSY AND I DON'T WANT ANY COOKIES, MAGAZINES... LAMPS, OR WHATEVER ELSE YOU'RE PEDDLING.
I'M HERE INVESTIGATING THE HAUNTING OF THE HOME OF HENRY AND WANDA BROOKS.
AH, I SEE. PLEASE, COME IN.

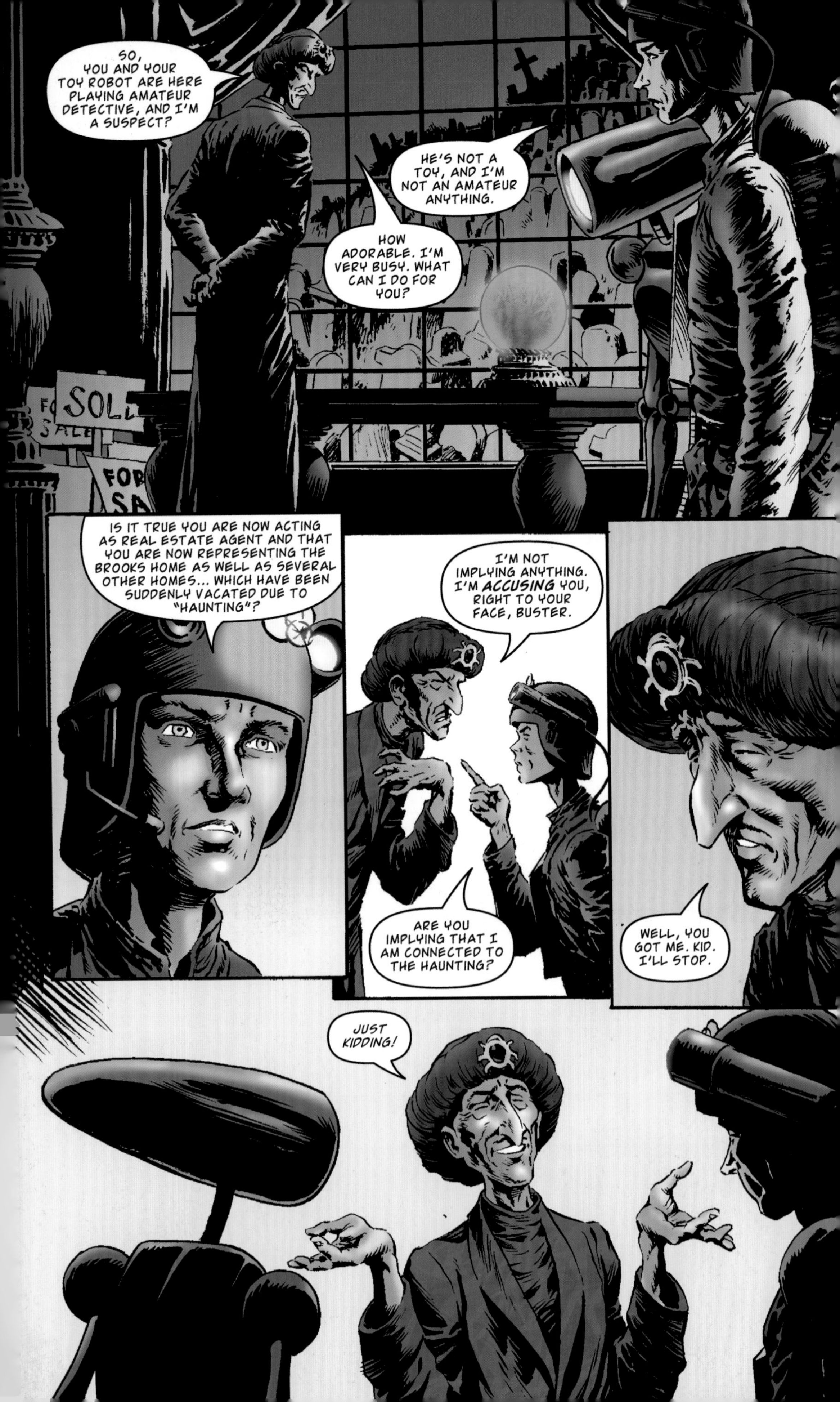
SO, YOU AND YOUR TOY ROBOT ARE HERE PLAYING AMATEUR DETECTIVE, AND I'M A SUSPECT?
HE'S NOT A TOY, AND I'M NOT AN AMATEUR ANYTHING.
HOW ADORABLE. I'M VERY BUSY. WHAT CAN I DO FOR YOU?
SOLD
FOR SALE
IS IT TRUE YOU ARE NOW ACTING AS REAL ESTATE AGENT AND THAT YOU ARE NOW REPRESENTING THE BROOKS HOME AS WELL AS SEVERAL OTHER HOMES... WHICH HAVE BEEN SUDDENLY VACATED DUE TO "HAUNTING"?
ARE YOU IMPLYING THAT I AM CONNECTED TO THE HAUNTING?
I'M NOT IMPLYING ANYTHING. I'M *ACCUSING* YOU, RIGHT TO YOUR FACE, BUSTER.
WELL, YOU GOT ME. KID. I'LL STOP.
JUST KIDDING!

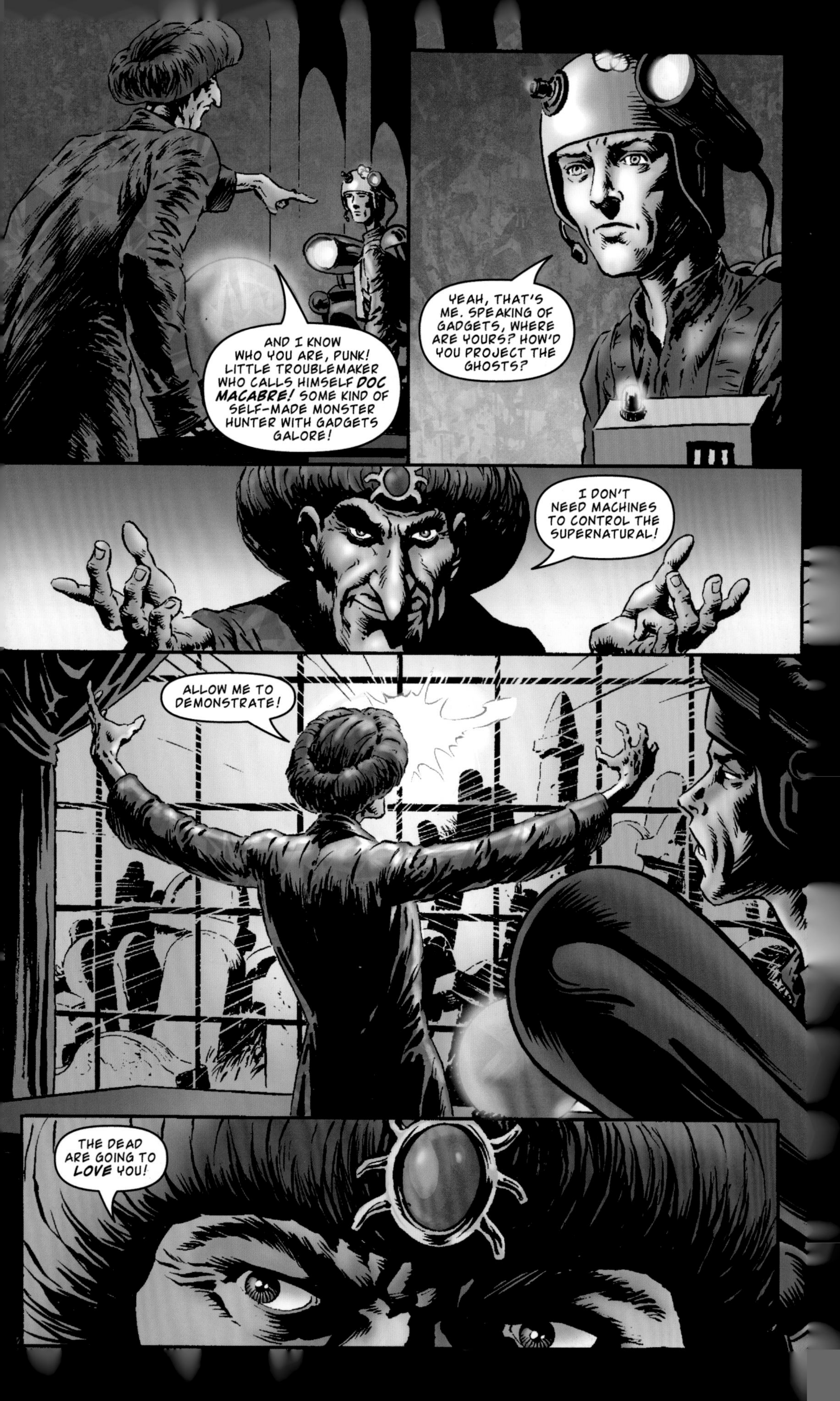
AND I KNOW WHO YOU ARE, PUNK! LITTLE TROUBLEMAKER WHO CALLS HIMSELF ***DOC MACABRE!*** SOME KIND OF SELF-MADE MONSTER HUNTER WITH GADGETS GALORE!
YEAH, THAT'S ME. SPEAKING OF GADGETS, WHERE ARE YOURS? HOW'D YOU PROJECT THE GHOSTS?
I DON'T NEED MACHINES TO CONTROL THE SUPERNATURAL!
ALLOW ME TO DEMONSTRATE!
THE DEAD ARE GOING TO ***LOVE*** YOU!

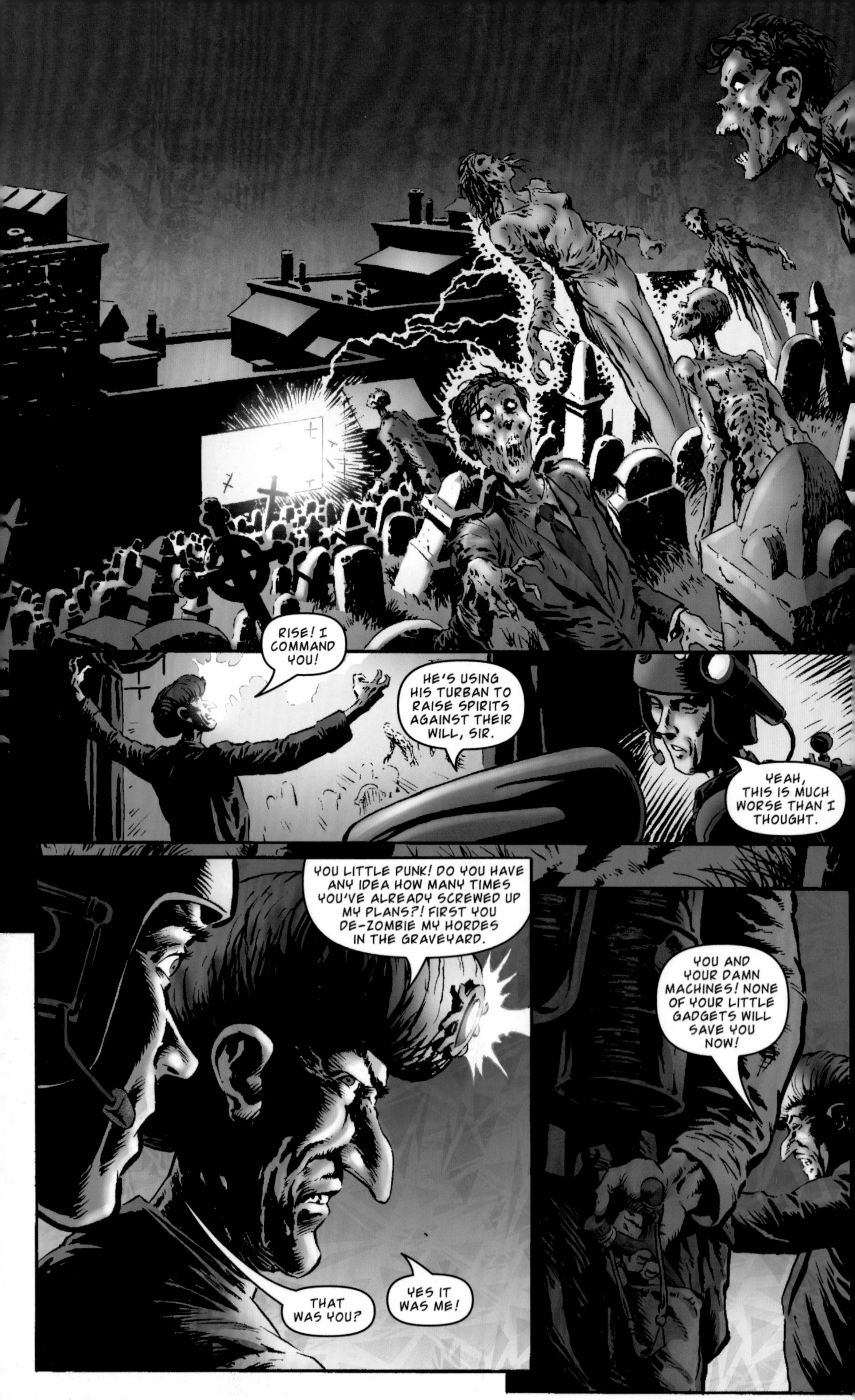

RISE! I COMMAND YOU!
HE'S USING HIS TURBAN TO RAISE SPIRITS AGAINST THEIR WILL, SIR.
YEAH, THIS IS MUCH WORSE THAN I THOUGHT.
YOU LITTLE PUNK! DO YOU HAVE ANY IDEA HOW MANY TIMES YOU'VE ALREADY SCREWED UP MY PLANS?! FIRST YOU DE-ZOMBIE MY HORDES IN THE GRAVEYARD.
THAT WAS YOU?
YES IT WAS ME!
YOU AND YOUR DAMN MACHINES! NONE OF YOUR LITTLE GADGETS WILL SAVE YOU NOW!

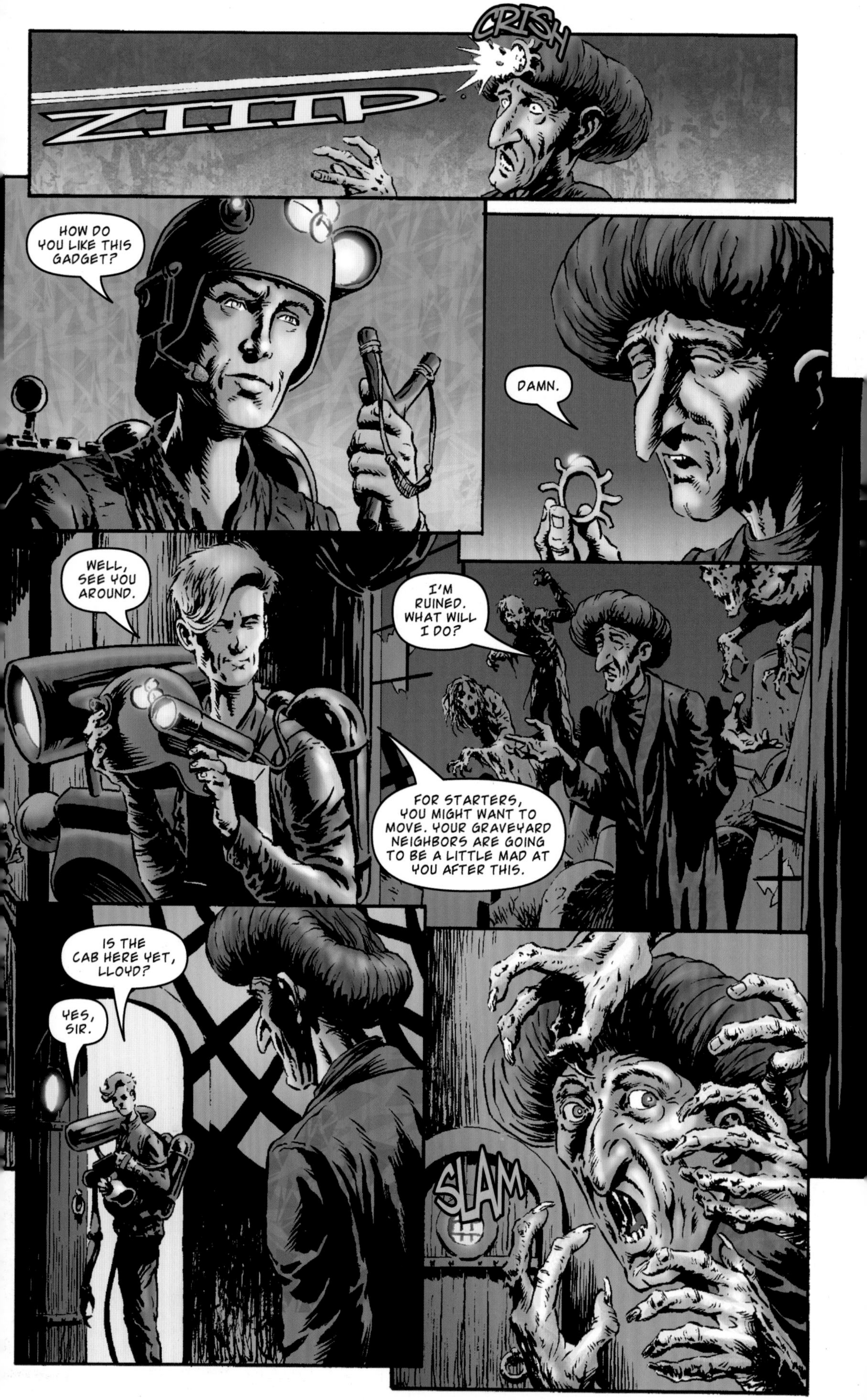
CRISH
ZIIIP
HOW DO YOU LIKE THIS GADGET?
DAMN.
WELL, SEE YOU AROUND.
I'M RUINED. WHAT WILL I DO?
FOR STARTERS, YOU MIGHT WANT TO MOVE. YOUR GRAVEYARD NEIGHBORS ARE GOING TO BE A LITTLE MAD AT YOU AFTER THIS.
IS THE CAB HERE YET, LLOYD?
YES, SIR.
SLAM

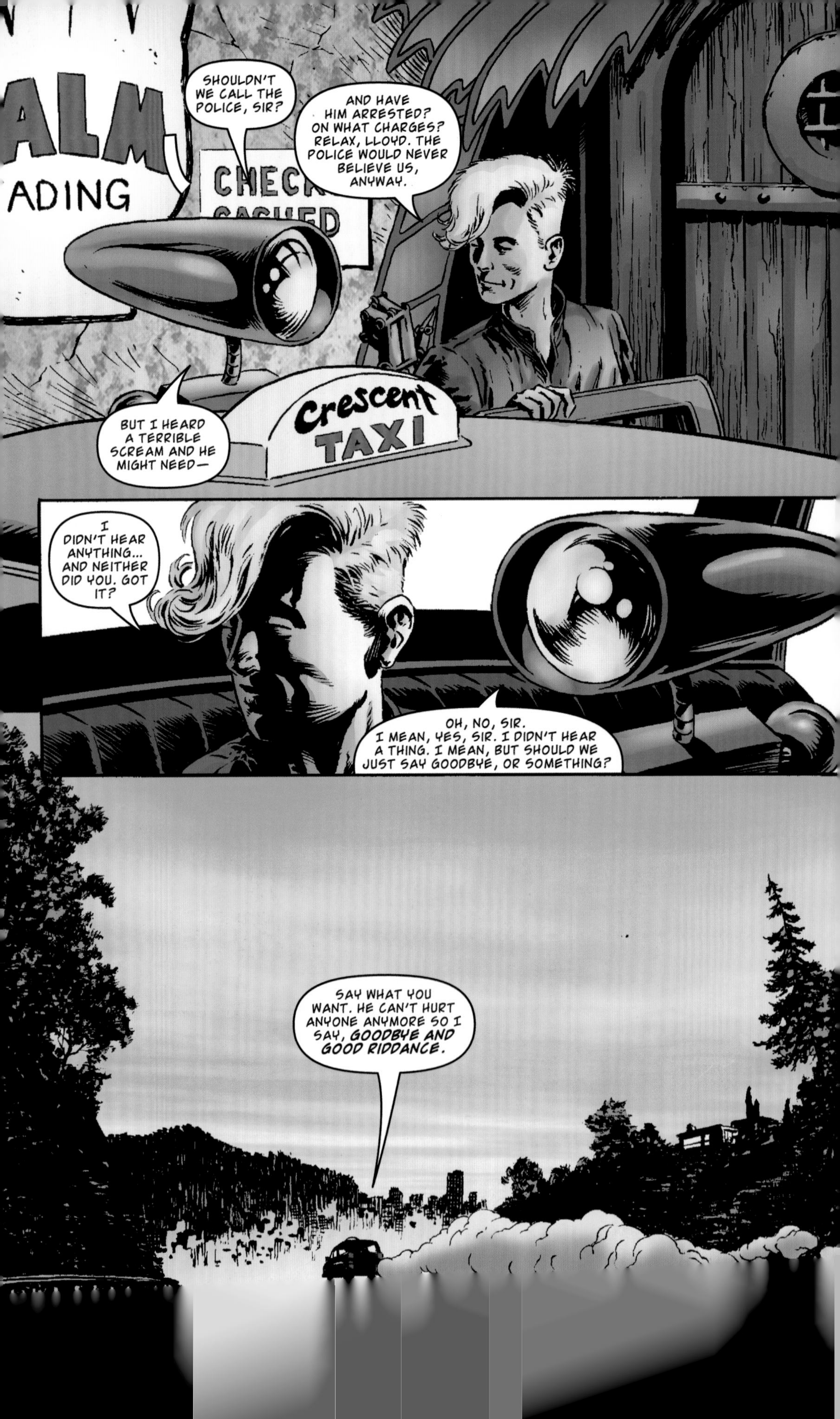
ALM
ADING
CHECK
SHOULDN'T WE CALL THE POLICE, SIR?
AND HAVE HIM ARRESTED? ON WHAT CHARGES? RELAX, LLOYD. THE POLICE WOULD NEVER BELIEVE US, ANYWAY.
BUT I HEARD A TERRIBLE SCREAM AND HE MIGHT NEED—
Crescent TAXI
I DIDN'T HEAR ANYTHING... AND NEITHER DID YOU. GOT IT?
OH, NO, SIR. I MEAN, YES, SIR. I DIDN'T HEAR A THING. I MEAN, BUT SHOULD WE JUST SAY GOODBYE, OR SOMETHING?
SAY WHAT YOU WANT. HE CAN'T HURT ANYONE ANYMORE SO I SAY, ***GOODBYE AND GOOD RIDDANCE***.

EXCLUSIVE INTERVIEW WITH
DOC MACABRE

Who is Doc Macabre? That's the question you hear all over town these days. The cops want to know, that's for sure, and so does the district attorney, the mayor, and, it turns out, my editor. As for me, well, I started the week not caring one bit about the "Mystery Man of Los Angeles" because the whole thing sounded like a Halloween hoax and I outgrew Ouija boards a long time ago. It's not the guys in the morgue that scare me, it's the ones sitting in county lock-up—and worse, the ones smoking cigars at City Hall. But my editor cares about Doc Macabre and that means I have to play along just like I do when the trick-or-treat crowd bangs on my door looking for a sugar fix.

A guy I know at the cemetery owes me a favor (don't ask—seriously) so I get a phone number. I call and ask for Macabre and I get someone who sounds like his son. I arrange a time and place to meet—I pick Charlie Walker's Tavern in Hollywood, a place with brown leather booths and shoe-polish coffee. In walks the guy I want to meet and I can't believe it when I see him. I was expecting Boris Karloff and I get Opie Taylor.

Q: You're just a kid, I thought you would be older. I thought you were, I don't know, a doctor?

A. I hear that a lot. I'm afraid my body and mind have always been a little out of sync. The Doctor label is something I took on because no creature of the night would fear "Chad Martin," you know? This is why I took the name "Doc" and not doctor. I have many degrees, but I don't carry the official title of doctor.

Q: To strike fear in the hearts of the superstitious bad guys?

A. No, it just sounds cool.

Q: So, how old are you, exactly?

A: I'd rather not say exactly, but not old enough to get a driver's license. My whole life, my age has been an issue and I'd rather not make too big a deal about it now. As you may or may not know, I am the youngest to

have ever graduated from M.I.T., as I started college while most kids my age were in elementary school.

Q: How did you get along with children your own age?

A: Not very well, I'm afraid. I was viewed as a freak among them. The limited time I spent with kids my age was extremely unpleasant. You know how children can be cruel. I was a prime target. I understand that now. What confounded me were the older students I met at the various institutes I attended. My older classmates, most of them at least, wanted nothing to do with me. I found out later they were mad because I was upsetting the grading curve.

Q: Right, I'm sure. So... are the good people of Los Angeles actually supposed to believe that there are zombies and ghosts and vampires actually prowling our sidewalks and canyons?

A: People can believe what they like, but the facts are the facts. The truth is that just about everything we believe to be legend has some particle of fact to it. There are ghosts, yes, but they are not always what we traditionally call ghosts. I have encountered spirits extracted from graves via technology, as well as the more typical poltergeists. Zombies are very real and extremely dangerous because they spread their own disease. Containment is very important. I have also encountered the more traditional zombie from Voodoo lore and they can be quite dangerous themselves, mostly because living humans control them. And yes, there are vampires, as many varieties of bloodsucker as we have fish in the sea. Very few modern vampires seem to be affected by the traditional killing methods; cross, holy water… all of that has passed. I suppose monsters must become as modernized as any of us.

Q: Where are your parents? What do they think of all this?

A: I'm sorry, but in order to protect them, I do not discuss my parents. I will say, however, that they were, and remain, very supportive of me, and the life I've chosen to pursue. They would like it if I met a girl, but… well, that's not really something I have control over, is it?

Q: Over at the police department there are some guys in the lab who want to talk to you about some blood they've found; they can't quite decide if it's human or not. Then there are some guys in the fraud unit, too, that want to know what you're charging people for…

A: I have a peaceful relationship with the police department. The fact is I handle cases that they do not want to deal with, so despite their public grumbling about my being a vigilante, I believe they support what

I do. I did have a chance to analyze the blood the police came into, but they were not happy when I told them that, as you said, it was not human blood.

Q: What was it?

A: Lycanthrope blood. Werewolves are fairly easy to detect. They are not very smart when in animal form, and unlike vampires, there are only a handful of breeds.

Q: Oh, well—that clears everything up. What's the scariest thing you've ever seen?

A: I was just getting started when I was asked to help on a case of a haunted asylum. It was a basic haunting; tortured souls trapped where they most likely died and trying to have vengeance on the living. This case was no different. I was able to free the ghosts, but I had to find their bodies first. I used a sonar device and found over a hundred small skeletons beneath the building. That was the worst.

Q: So what's a normal day for you? You don't seem like a kid who plays Wii or watches "iCarly." "Scooby-Doo" re-runs, maybe…

A: I am fascinated with the current explosion of technological distractions, but I don't have time to use them much. The one time I played a videogame I wound up sitting there for 17 hours until I

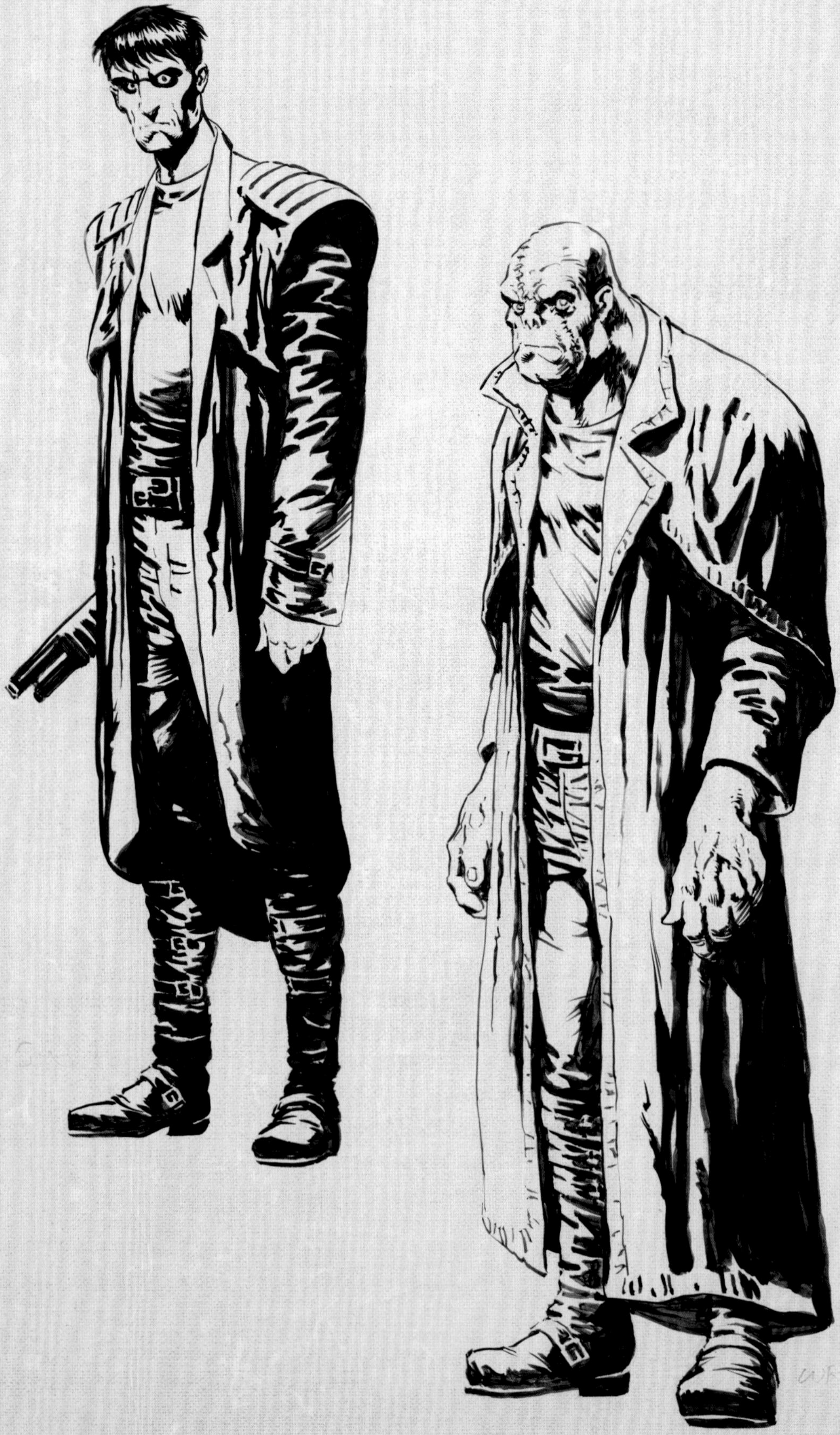

finished the game's quest. I can't risk that happening again so I do not have any game systems in the laboratory.

Q: Well, I think you're the weirdest kid I've ever met and just maybe the most dangerous person in Los Angeles. I got one last question for you—for now: What do you want to be when you grow up, Doc Macabre?

A: [Laughs] I am what I want to be when I grow up… a monster hunter!

And with that the kid finishes his Sprite, puts a stack of coins on the table, and heads out onto the sidewalks of Los Angeles, a city with four million living souls and, apparently, a good number of undead ones, too. I sat there and stared at my notes and a horrible thought crossed my mind. Does this mean my mother-in-law—who we put in the ground three years ago—might show up one morning looking even scarier than she did with a beating heart? The waitress came by to refill my coffee but I covered the cup with my palm. "Let's replace that with a gin and tonic," I told her.

Next: Doc Macabre discusses recent cases and how he knows The Ghoul!

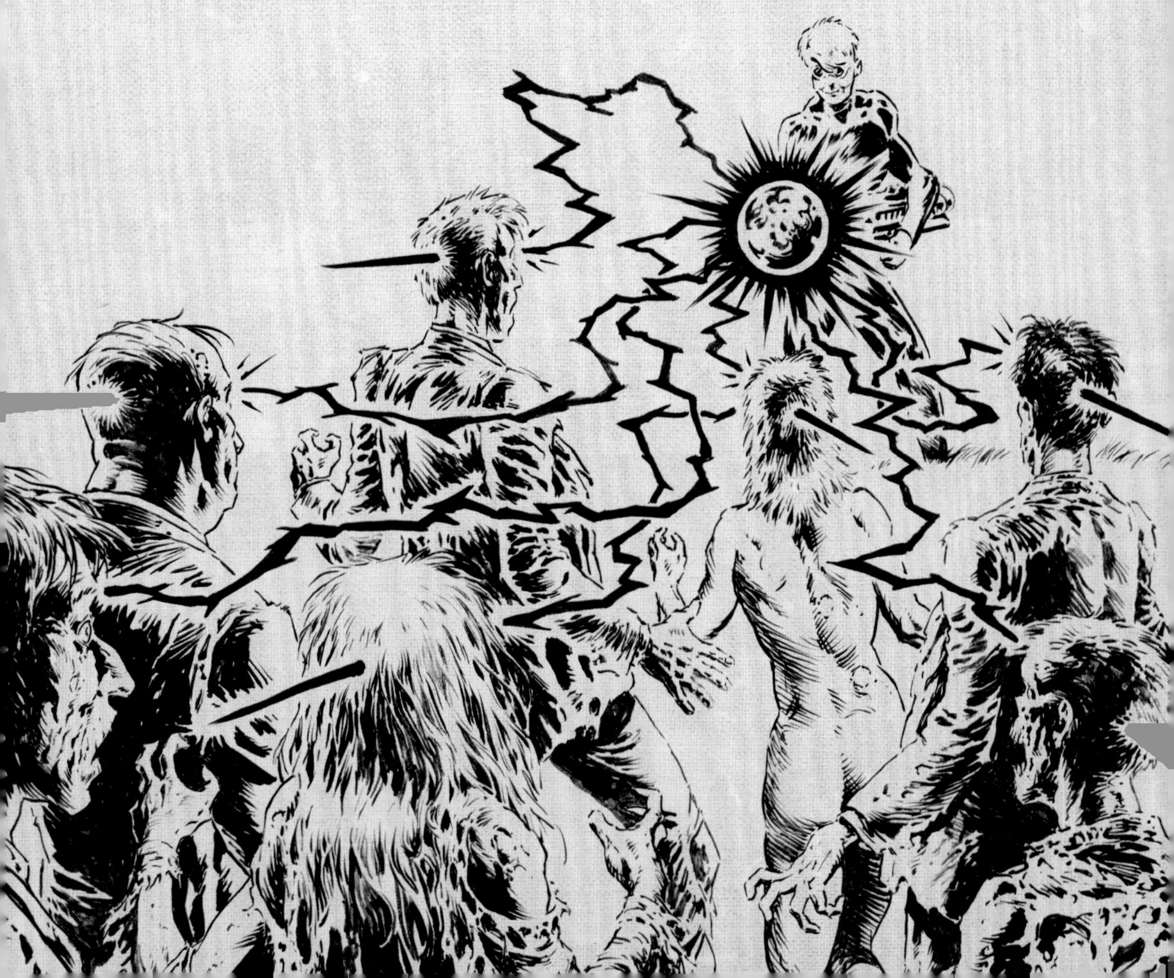

Doc Macabre in "The Ghoul."

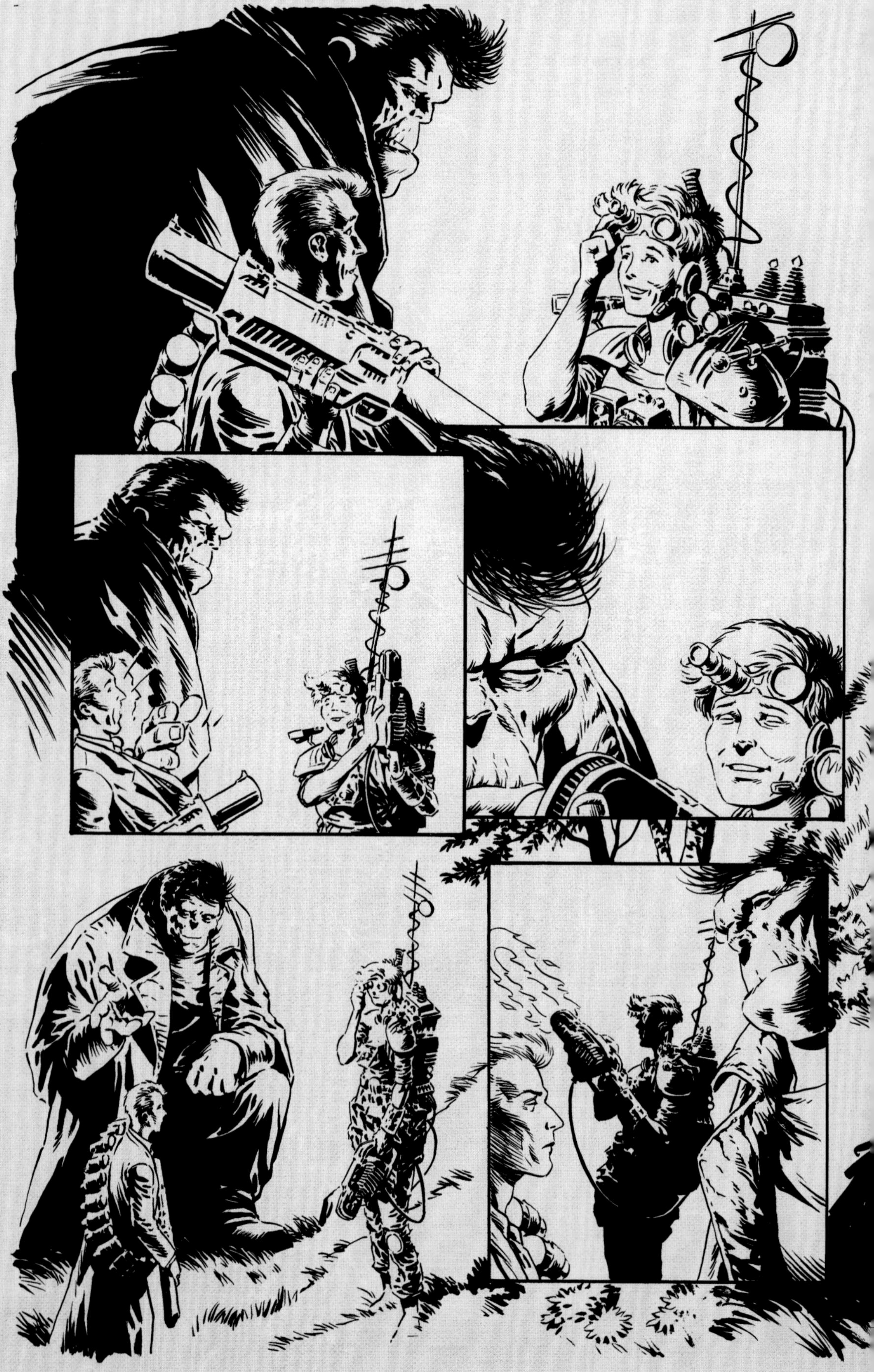

EXCLUSIVE INTERVIEW WITH
DOC MACABRE

In our last installment, we talked to Doc Macabre a little about what makes him who he is. Today we're going to ask Doc about some of his past exploits, including his rumored association with The Ghoul and the mysterious detective named Coogan.

One immediately notices, while talking to Doc Macabre, that he is very much a young boy in many ways—for lunch, he had chicken tenders and mac and cheese—but at the same time, he carries himself like an adult. I was instantly struck by the thoughtfulness of his answers, and how much he truly cared about his life's passion.

D oc is what so many of us dreamed of becoming when we were children. He is a self-made monster hunter, spiritualist, and ghost chaser. And yet, while talking about the atomic reactor he created when he was only nine years old, one can't help but smile at the cheddar cheese he has smeared below his nose. Genius, yes—but still only a kid.

Q: Can you tell us how you came to meet The Ghoul?

Doc Macabre: That is kind of an amusing story, actually. It was when I first started out. I was just a kid at the time. I mean, I was a really little kid. I'd just invented a device that could create a protective body shield out of pure, simple electricity. I believe The Ghoul was still working for the government at the time, and they sent him to talk to me about acquiring the device for the FBI.

Q: How did that first meeting go?

Doc Macabre: Have you ever seen The Ghoul? I was terrified! I thought the Frankenstein Monster was after me. Honestly, looking back, I think how stupid the Feds were to send a giant monster-man after a child. I mean, send a note, right? But, anyway, I thought I was being hunted, and like any smart human who's seen at least one horror movie, I was very aware that, when a monster chases you, you run!

Q: How long did you run?

Doc Macabre: It was only a few hours, but I managed to lure The Ghoul to the city sewage treatment plant. I tested the force field on myself—luckily it worked, at least long enough to allow me to shove The Ghoul into the raw sewage. He was so mad, and I couldn't stop laughing because every time he tried to yell at me, he'd get a whiff of himself and throw up. He spent the better part of an hour yelling at me and puking. I laughed so hard I peed… which shorted out the force field device and I was given a very nasty electric shock.

Q: And somehow you forged a working relationship with The Ghoul, right?

Doc Macabre: He's helped me out on several occasions, and I have helped him. We have talked about doing more work together now that he has left the FBI. I always have trouble with government agencies. They always try to steal my inventions.

Q: If you had to choose one invention of yours, what would be your favorite?

Doc Macabre: I'd have to say Lloyd is my favorite invention. He is just a simple robot assistant, but his AI has surprised me, specifically his ability to adapt and learn. He's developed a very likable personality, which I'd like to take credit for, but in all honesty was a complete accident.

Q: I hope you don't mind my pointing it out, but when you talk about Lloyd, you sound like you're talking about a friend, not a machine you built.

Doc Macabre: I suppose I have come to think of him as more of a friend than something I created. It's amazing that we live in a world where something like that is even possible.

Q: Back up a little. Would you care to elaborate on why you choose not to sell your patents to other agencies like the FBI or U.S. Army?

Doc Macabre: It's very simple, actually. I create inventions that are specifically meant for use in dealing with supernatural situations. My inventions are not weapons, and I'm afraid these agencies would use the creations for evil instead of good. I know it's a terrible cliché, but it is how I feel.

Q: Has there ever been an invention you created that completely backfired?

Doc Macabre: (laughs) More than once!

Q: Care to elaborate?

Doc Macabre: The worst was when I created a machine that was meant to increase my size, but instead it did just the opposite. I spent a week in the lab no taller than a stickpin. Luckily, Lloyd found me before the cat did.

Q: Is that device still in use today?

Doc Macabre: Yes, I use it to shrink my garbage to microscopic size. I only have to take out the trash every six months that way.

Q: I found it very interesting that, despite being very private, you've allowed, of all things, a comic book to be done about you. What made you decide to do that?

Doc Macabre: I was approached by a friend, and they explained that doing a comic would be a good way to introduce me—and what I do— to the world. I haven't had much

luck with the mainstream media—present company excluded, of course—so I thought allowing my adventures to be told in comic form might yield better results.

Q: Do you read comics?

Doc Macabre: I did when I was younger. I don't really have time to now. These days I mainly listen to books on tape while I work. I just listened to the first novel by Stephen King's kid. It was very good. I can't wait to read his second. I hear he does comics, too… something about a padlock? I forget.

Q: The publisher got a great creative team for your book, too. Are you happy about that? They got Steve Niles to do the writing.

Doc Macabre: I'm afraid I've never heard of him.

Q: And Bernie Wrightson doing the art.

Doc Macabre: Now, him I've heard of. That is very exciting. Mr. Wrightson is a legend. I love his **Frankenstein** and, of course, his **Swamp Thing**.

Q: But you've never heard of the writer?

Doc Macabre: No. Sorry.

Q: They did a film based on one of his comics.

Doc Macabre: **Kick-Ass**? I enjoyed that one.

Q: No. It was about vampires.

Doc Macabre: I'm sick of vampires… in films and real life.

Q: You've encountered a vampire in real life?

Doc Macabre: More than once. If people knew how infested L.A. is with vampires, there would be a mass exodus like the one following the Northridge Quake. I'd have to say that vampires are my least favorite monster to hunt. They are dirty, filthy creatures, who carry and spread disease… and bad taste. Really, they are the human equivalent of rats. Nasty creatures.

Q: Filthier than, say, zombies?

Doc Macabre: Zombies are filthy, but they are also witless idiots, so they are easily dispatched. Vampires are like zombies with massive egos. They are just a (excuse my language) pain in the ass to deal with.

Q: Is that why you specialize in ghosts?

Doc Macabre: Ghosts just fascinate me. I believe ghosts carry the secrets that can bridge science with the supernatural. They are, after all, remnants of people who are bound to earth. I think we can learn a great deal from spirits if we learn how to contact them correctly.

Q: You sound more interested in studying ghosts than in hunting them.

Doc Macabre: That's true, and for good reason. Ghosts are not always bad. They are often confused and their actions, as a result, often seem hostile to the living. But it's very rare that you find an actual evil spirit. Most of the time, ghosts are simply trapped in a certain place and need a little guidance finding their way.

Q: But there are bad ghosts?

Doc Macabre: When bad people die, they become bad ghosts. So, yes, they are out there. I've battled some major jerk ghosts over the years. But my hope is to one day find a way to meet and talk with the spirits of the dead so we can learn more from them.

Q: There's another person you've been linked to here in LA. Is it true you know Coogan, the detective who passed away several years ago?

Doc Macabre: (laughs) How could I know a dead man?

Q: Some say he didn't really die.

Doc Macabre: I'm really not at liberty to say anything. As far as I know, Detective Coogan was shot and killed by an assassin's bullet. Rumors of his continuing detecting after his death are just that—rumors.

Q: Can you tell our readers anything about what you are working on now?

Doc Macabre: I usually have a few things going at once. As a matter of fact, I have several ongoing cases right now, but I'm afraid I can't discuss them. I also have several inventions in the pipeline, but my main focus has been upgrading Lloyd.

Q: Upgrading?

Doc Macabre: Lloyd was only the third robot I've ever built. I've learned much more since he was constructed, so I'm adding some new features. I've learned how to construct functional legs, so I'm removing his wheels. I'm also looking into new arms, as well as a variety of other new functions.

Q: Upgrading your friend?

Doc Macabre: (laughs) Yes. I suppose it is funny when you think of it that way. There have been huge advances in robotics and artificial intelligence in just the last few years. I look forward to applying many of those advances to Lloyd as soon as possible.

This concludes Part 2 of the exclusive Doc Macabre interview. Tune in next month for the conclusion and a closer look at Doc Macabre's upbringing and life as a boy genius.

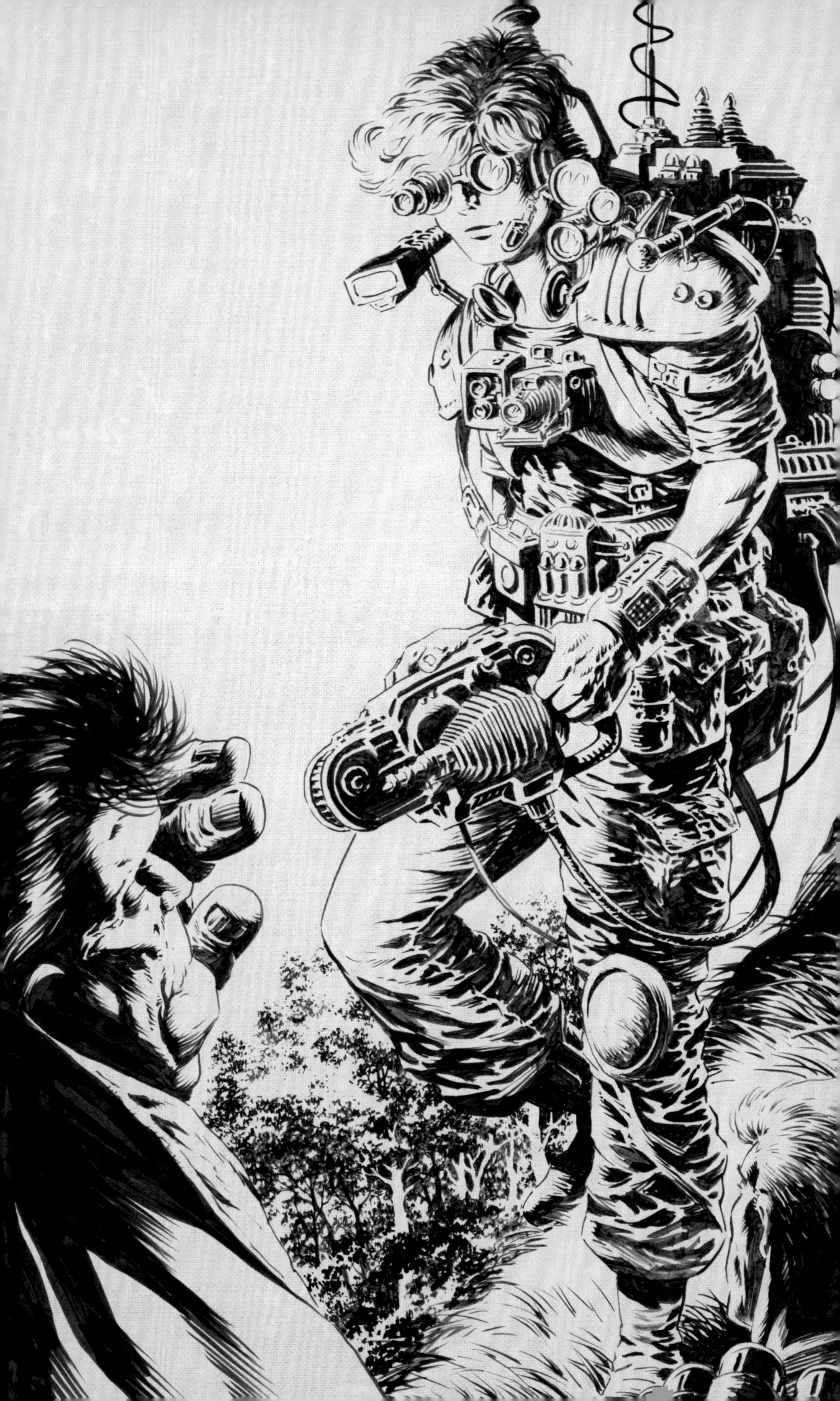

EXCLUSIVE INTERVIEW WITH
DOC MACABRE

In our third and final installment of our exclusive Doc Macabre one-on-one interview, the boy genius talks to us about the dangers of inventing, government intervention, paparazzi, and fills us in on one very big and surprising plan he has in the works!

For this last segment of the interview, Doc Macabre was kind enough to allow us into his secret lab (off Moorpark Ave) to have a look around and talk about the future.

Q: I can't help but notice, as I look around the lab, that most of your inventions look very, um—

Doc Macabre: Homemade? It's okay. I don't mind. I find that using everyday items to build my inventions works just as well as using new materials. Plus, I avoid the rip-off government prices on a lot of these things AND stay off their radar.

Q: Why do you need to stay off their radar?

Doc Macabre: Come now, we're all adults here… well, you are. I think we all know why the government would be interested in my work. But the fact is nothing I create can be perverted into some sort of weapons system. I am very careful to avoid that.

Q: But many of these devices I'm seeing certainly do look like weapons.

Doc Macabre: Weapons against the undead and ghosts. None of these could harm a human. I did create a device for re-inserting a ghost into its original body. But a slimy man in a black suit—asking if it could also remove the soul from a living person—approached me about it, and once I realized what he was asking, I immediately destroyed the device.

Q: What about the plans, the blueprints?

Doc Macabre: I write nothing down if I don't have to. The plans are in my head.

Note: While visiting Doc Macabre's lab I was introduced to Doc's robot assistant. His name is Lloyd, and he was kind enough to answer a few questions for us.

Q: What's it like assisting Doc Macabre?

Lloyd: It is fascinating work. I am hardwired to always be there for the Doc and do whatever he needs, but I think even if I wasn't programmed for it, I would still enjoy my work.

Q: So, you have a unique bond with your creator, then?

Lloyd: Not many have the fortune to meet and work with their creator. I consider myself very lucky. Doc Macabre is an extraordinary young man, and despite being my boss and creator, I have also come to regard him as my friend. I can only hope he feels the same way about me.

Q: Tell me what you think of the work you do, Lloyd? Do the types of investigations Doc and yourself work frighten you at all?

Lloyd: I am not programmed to be frightened. I can, however, detect high levels of danger, and there have been times working with the Doc I thought my motherboard would blow, but Doc always finds a way.

Q: Thank you, Lloyd.

Lloyd: My pleasure.

Q: Turning back to you, Doc. What's it like to spend most of your time talking to a robot of your own creation?

Doc Macabre: Ah, I see where you're going with this. I programmed Lloyd to be completely adaptable to his world. He is not loyal to me because he has to be. I programmed him with what I like to call Open AI. In simplest terms, if I treated Lloyd badly, he would not like me and most likely not do any work, either.

Q: Isn't that dangerous?

Doc Macabre: Only if I act like a jerk-hole.

Q: Interesting. Now there was a big fuss recently when an image of you, a photograph, surfaced and was published in the LA Times.

Doc Macabre: Yes. By Geoff Boucher. I saw that.

Q: You don't seem too happy about it.

Doc Macabre: I have gone to great lengths to stay under the radar and now all of my efforts have been threatened by amateur paparazzi. It's okay. I knew it would happen one day. I just wish the picture didn't look like a Bigfoot photo.

Q: So, you are willing to go public?
Doc Macabre: I suppose I can tell you this
now…
I have

been intending on going public. The photo just forced the issue. I have been working on a special project that would make my being public a necessity.

Q: Can you tell us about the project?

Doc Macabre: Yes, I suppose I should before someone else does. I have contacted Coogan (AKA The Dead Detective) and The Ghoul. I have suggested we pool our resources and form a team to use our combined knowledge and strength to take on supernatural evil.

Q: Wow. You guys will be a powerhouse. Do you have a name for the group?

Doc Macabre: Yes, we are calling ourselves THE MOORPARK REJECTS.

Q: This is amazing news. Any idea when we should expect to see the group working together?

Doc Macabre: No idea.

Q: You have a group, but you don't know when you're getting together?

Doc Macabre: Have you ever tried to organize a super-group? It's harder than you think. Plus, now everybody thinks we're having open auditions or something. Not to mention, The Ghoul is in Siberia right now—something about blood-sucking ice-giants.

Q: So, no idea when we might see the Moorpark Rejects in action?

Doc Macabre: As things stand right now, we are in a holding pattern. I spoke to Coogan last night. He's on a werewolf case currently. When he and The Ghoul are back, we'll have a meeting and see where things are.

Q: Any other possible members?

Doc Macabre: I got a call from a vampire who said he wanted to help us. I'm not sure how I feel about that. He appears honest enough, but vampires aren't exactly known for keeping their word.

Q: I think we've reached the end here, Doc. Thank you so much for allowing us to spend this time with you.

Doc Macabre: It was my pleasure.

Q: Anything you'd like to add or say to our readers?

Doc Macabre: I'd like to thank everybody from the bottom of my heart for the support they've shown me through tough times. And I assure everybody that I am keeping an eye out for evil spirits, and I will do everything in my power to ensure you are all safe.

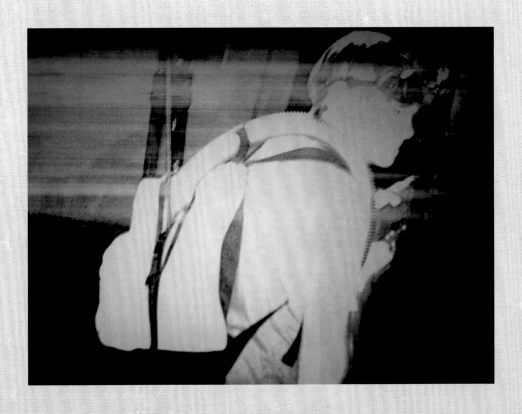

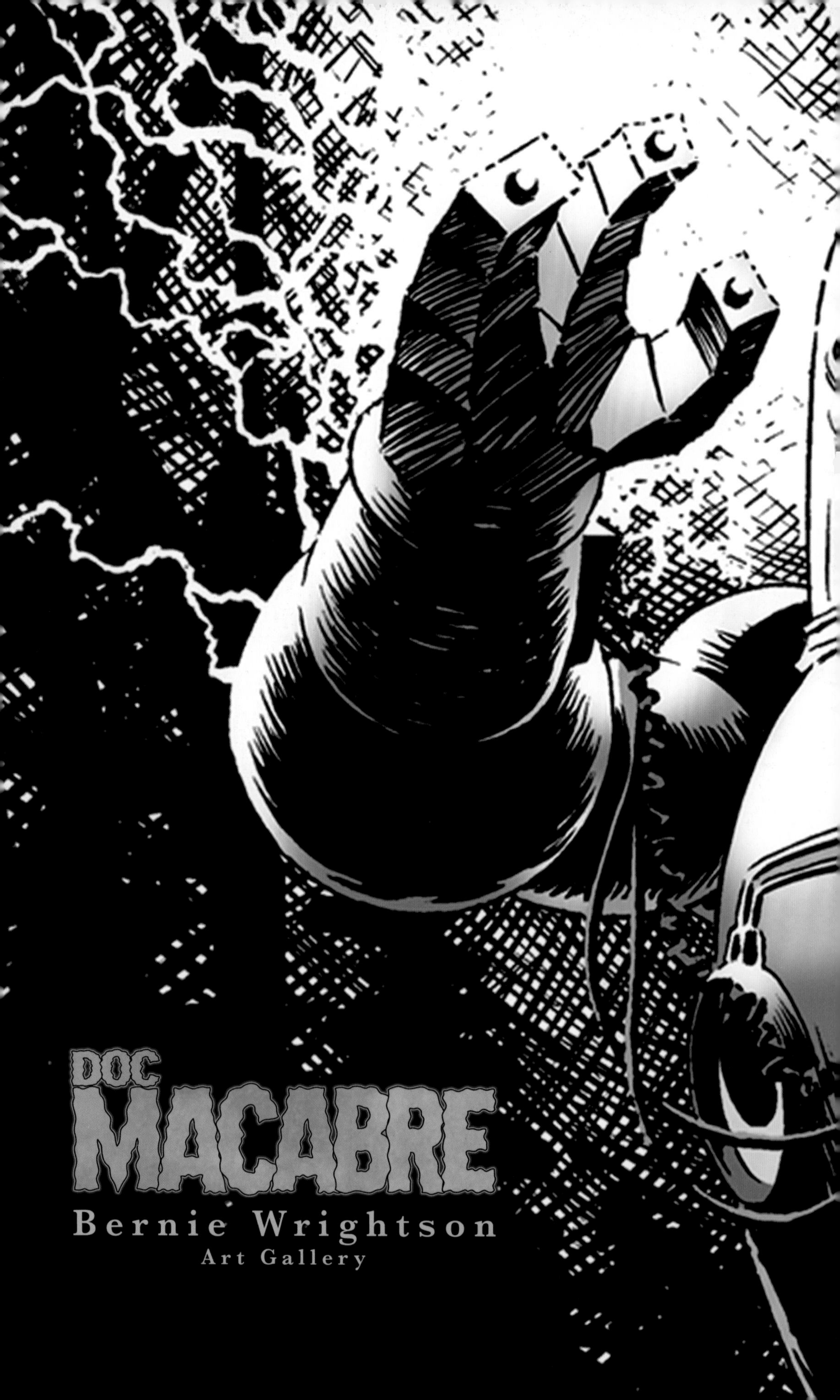
DOC
MACABRE
Bernie Wrightson
Art Gallery

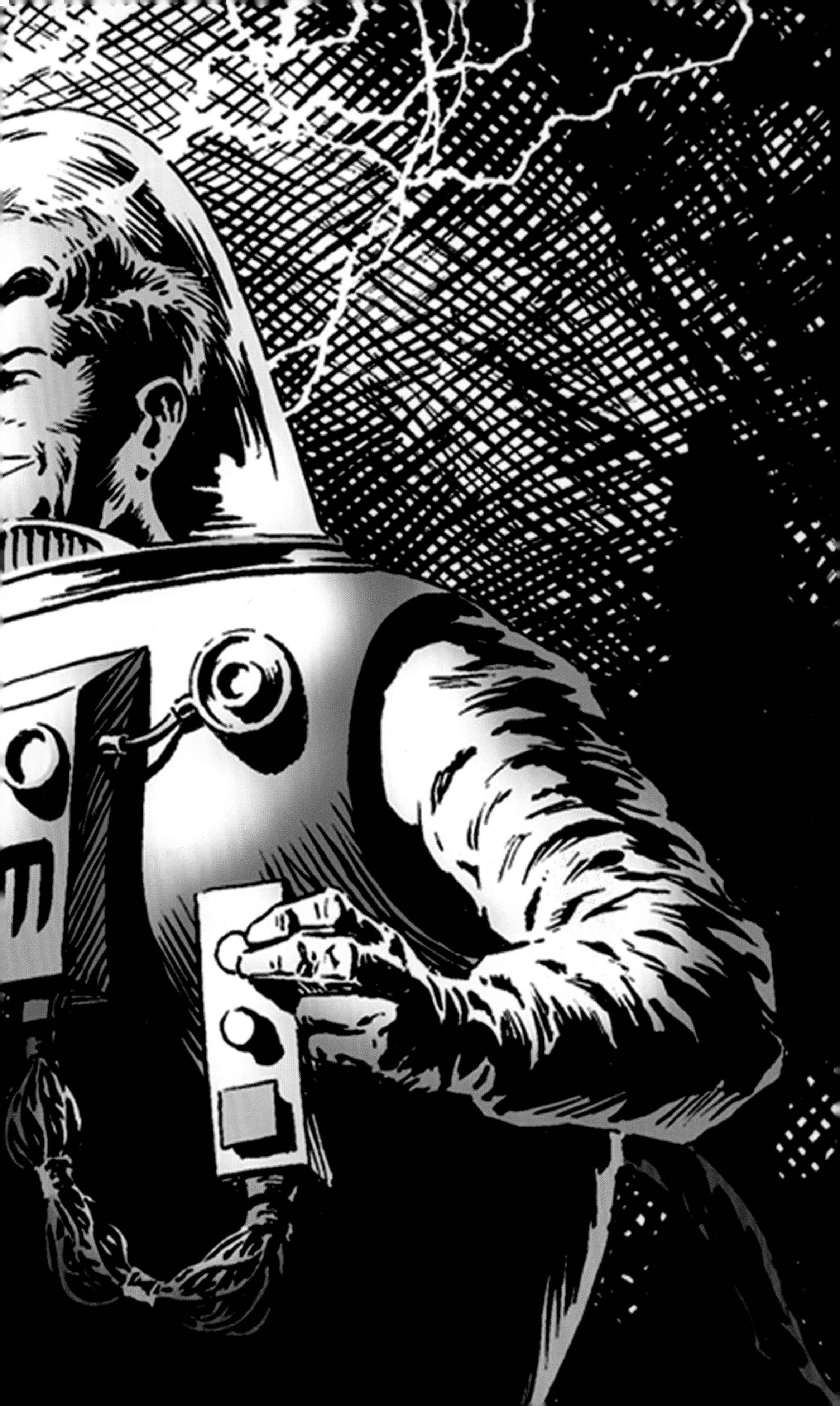

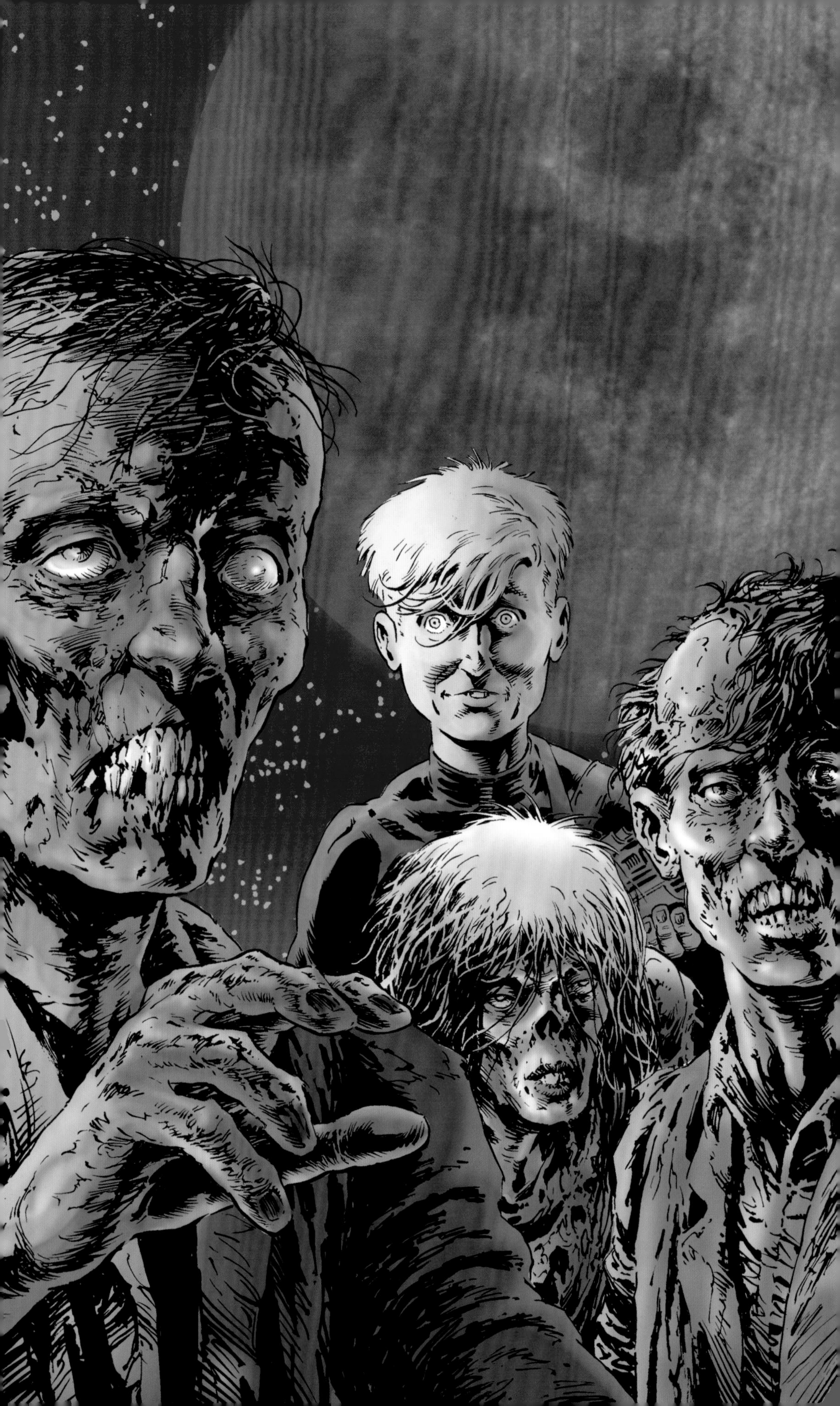

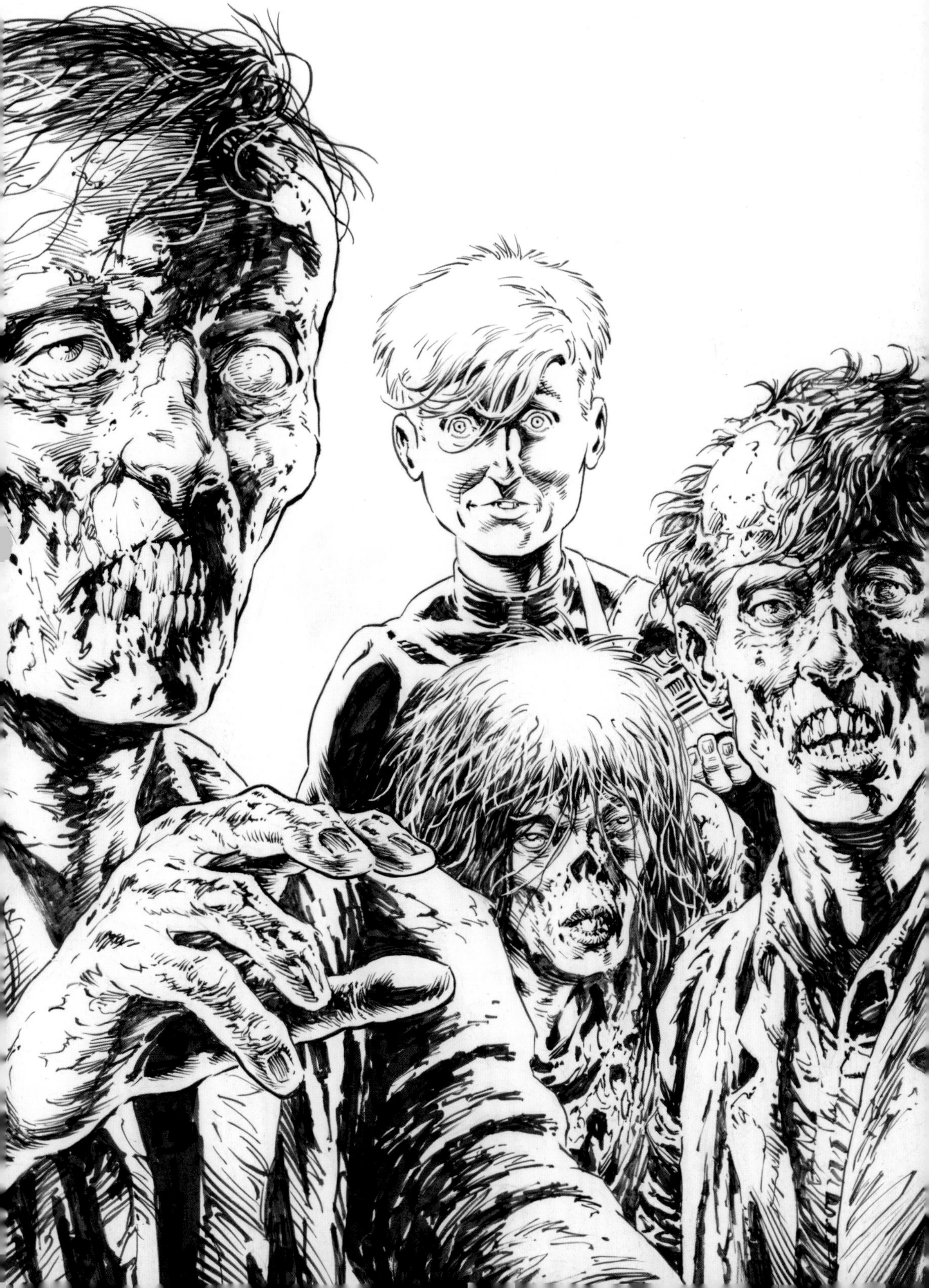

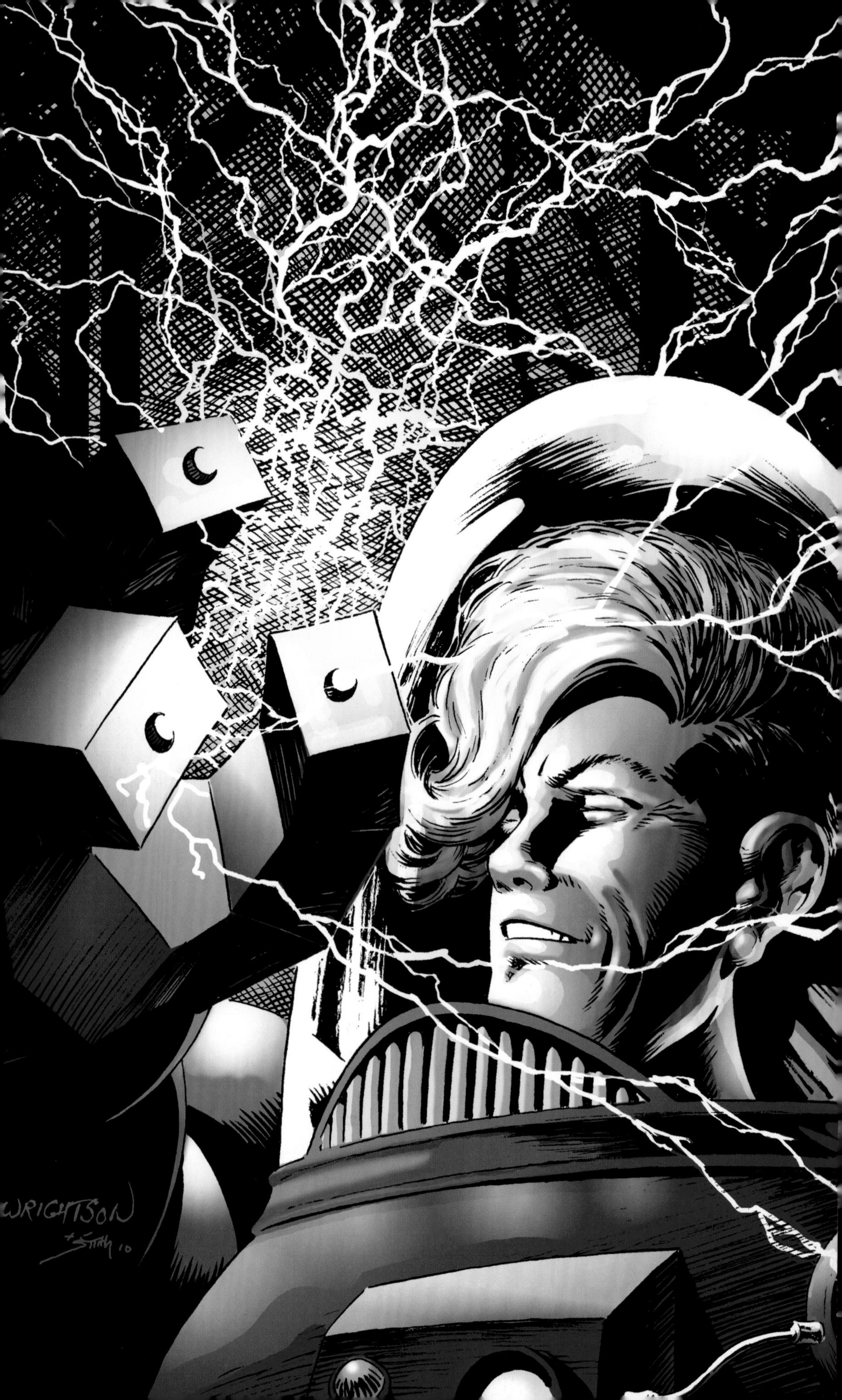
WRIGHTSON

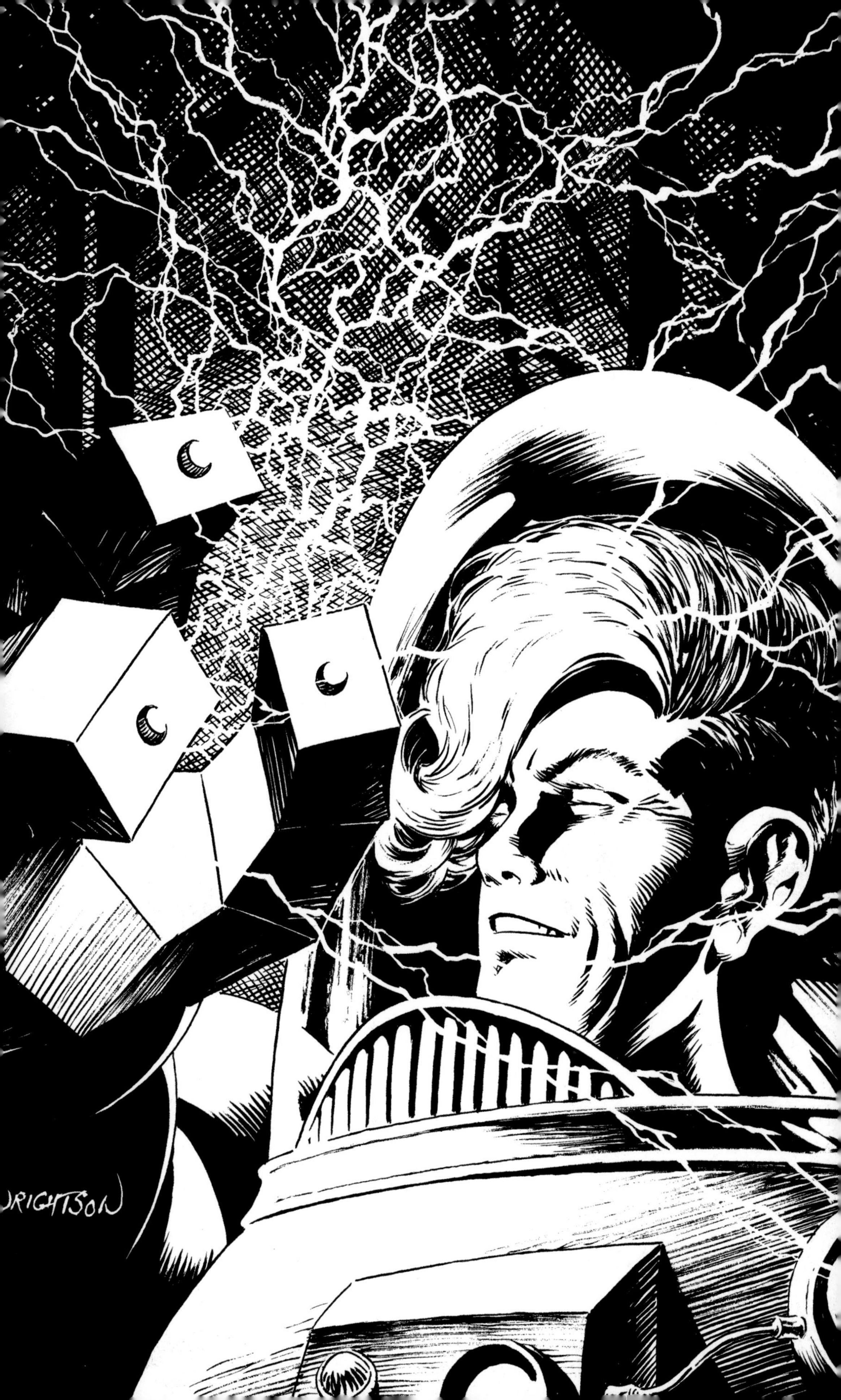

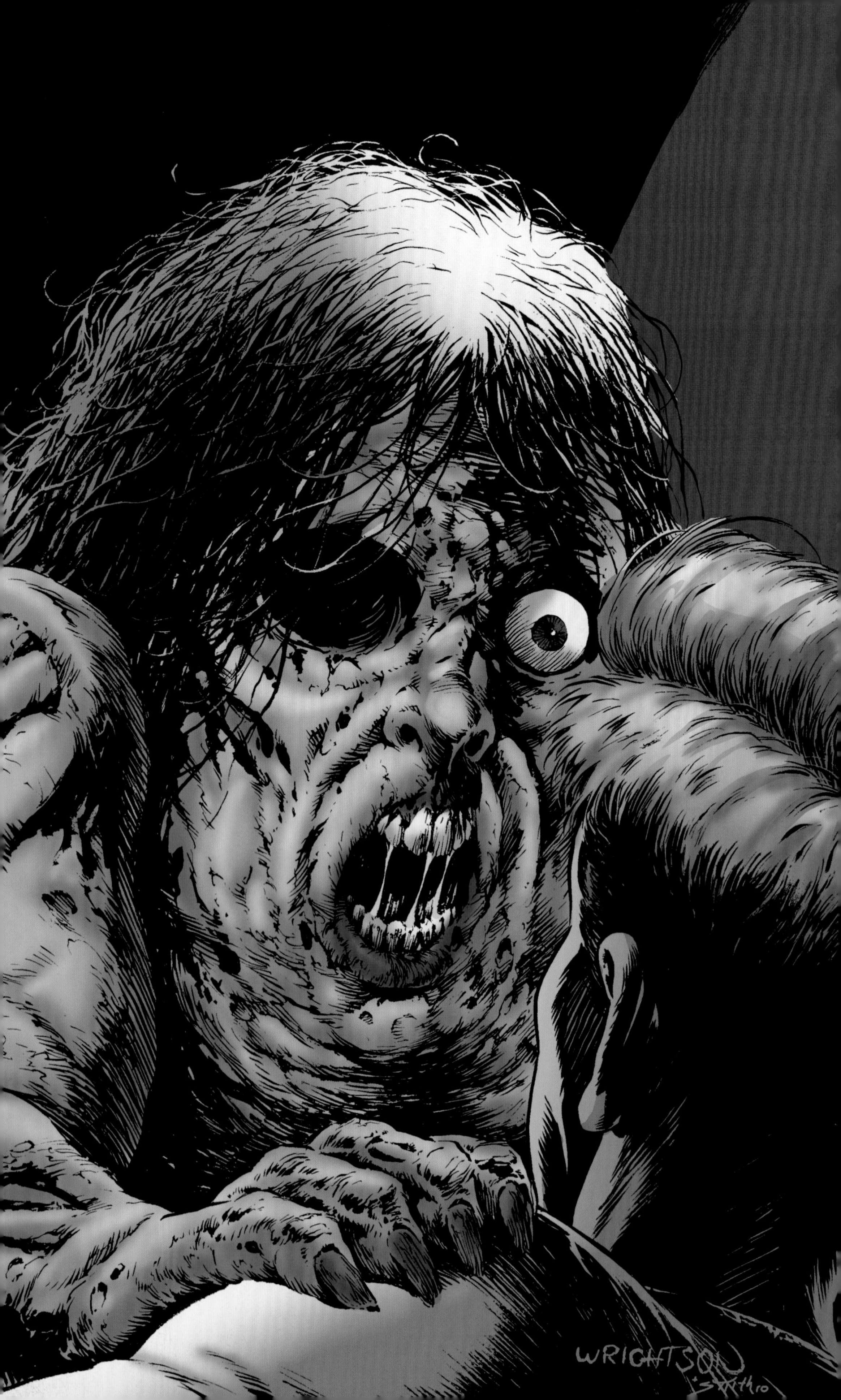
WRIGHTSON

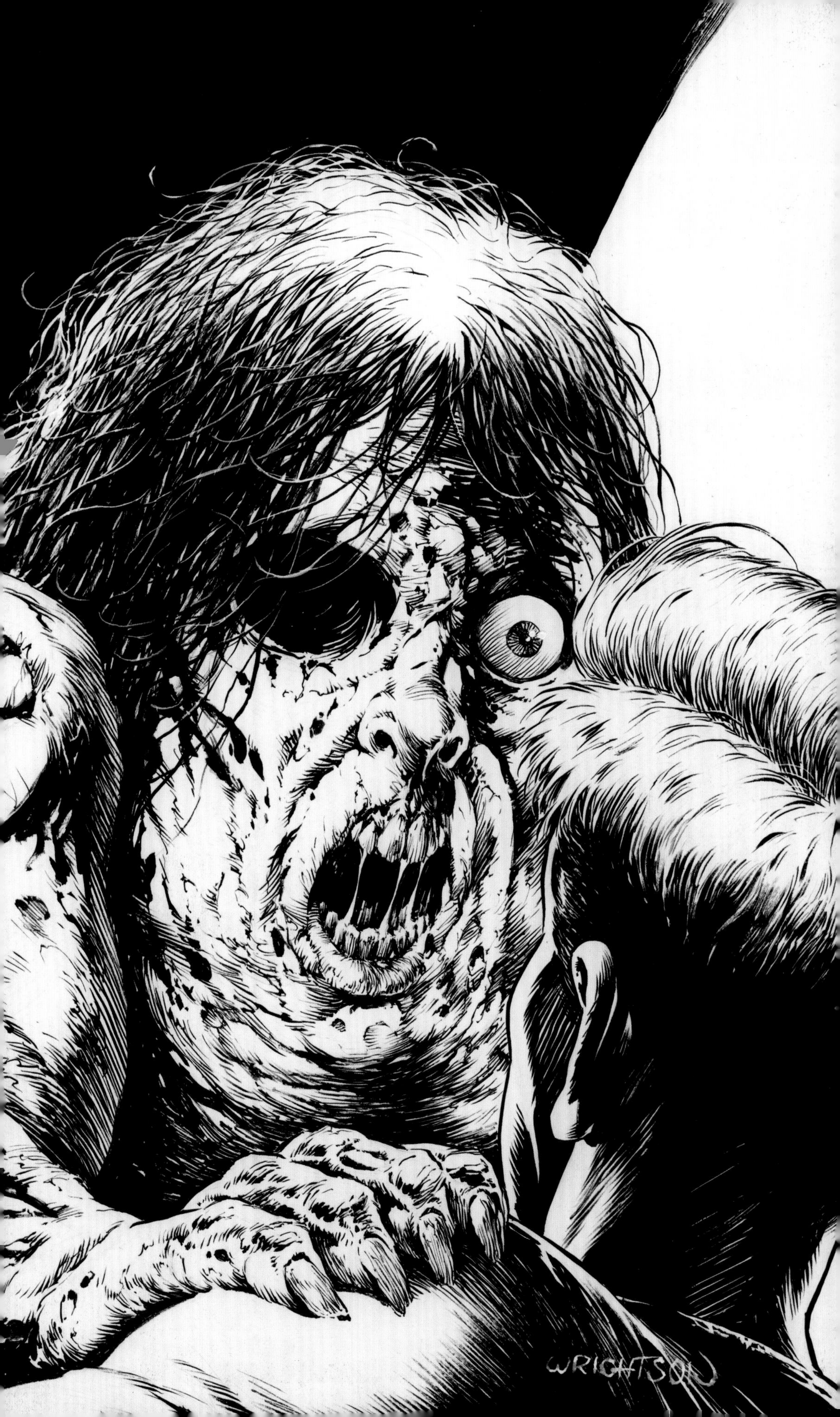
WRIGHTSON

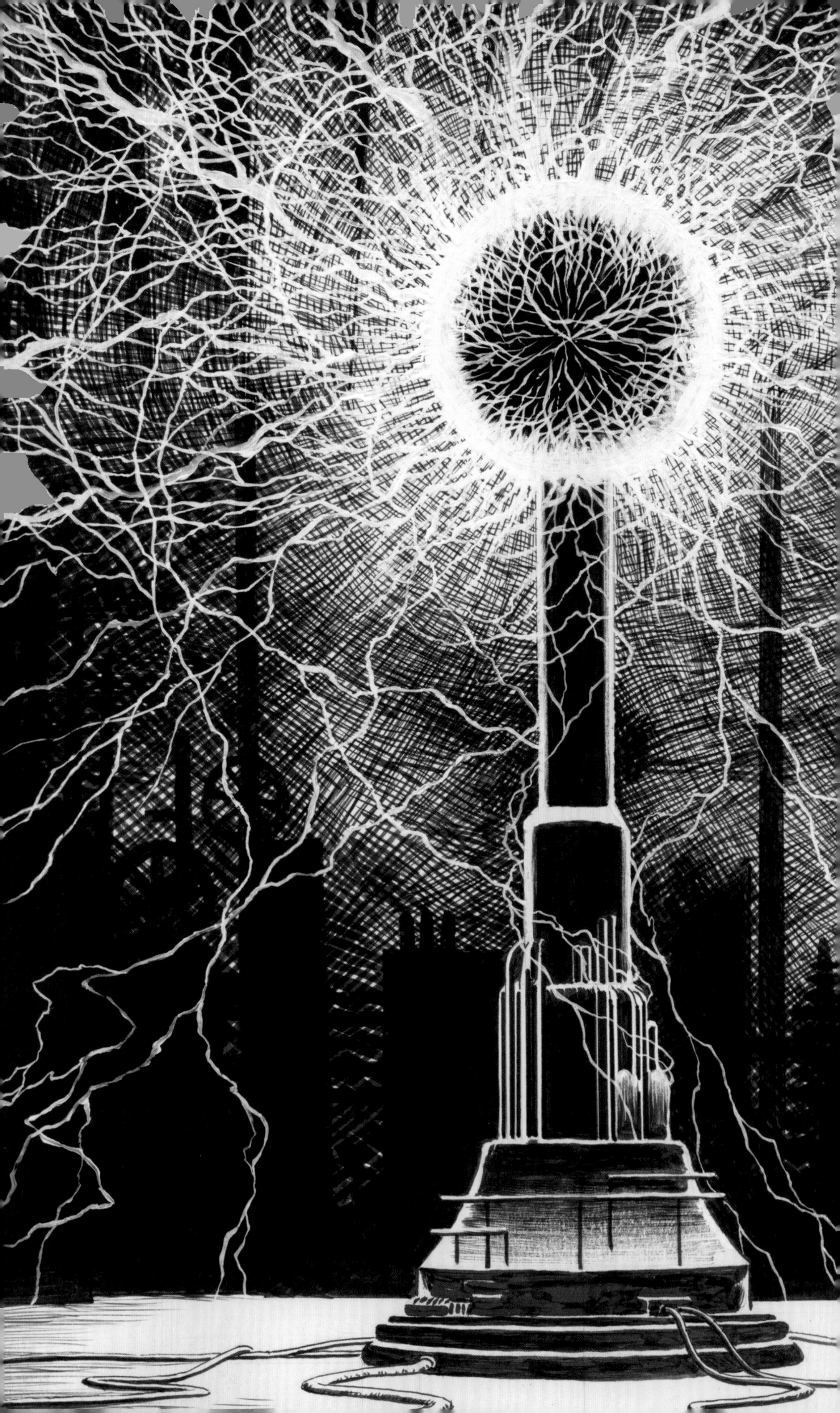

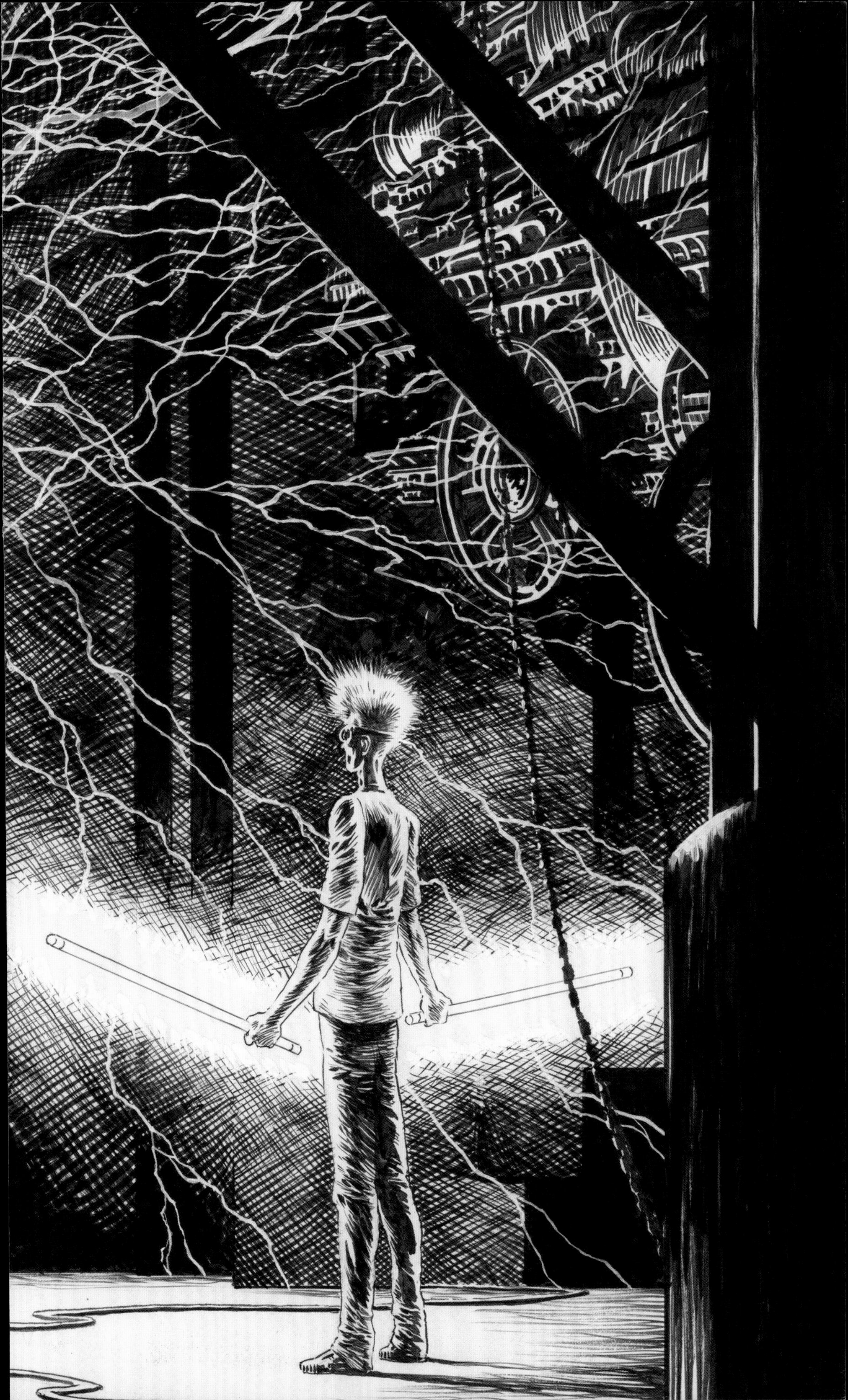

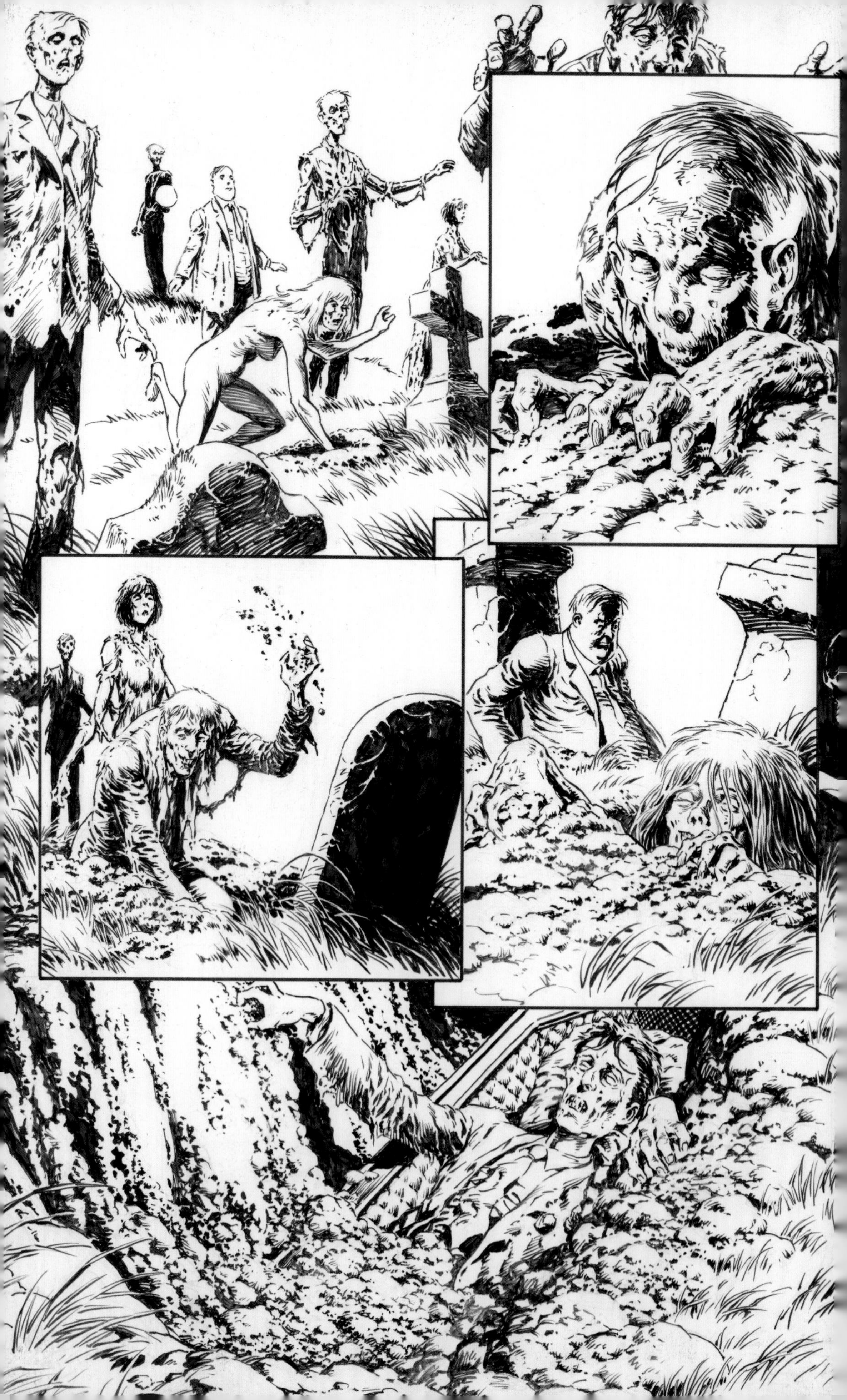

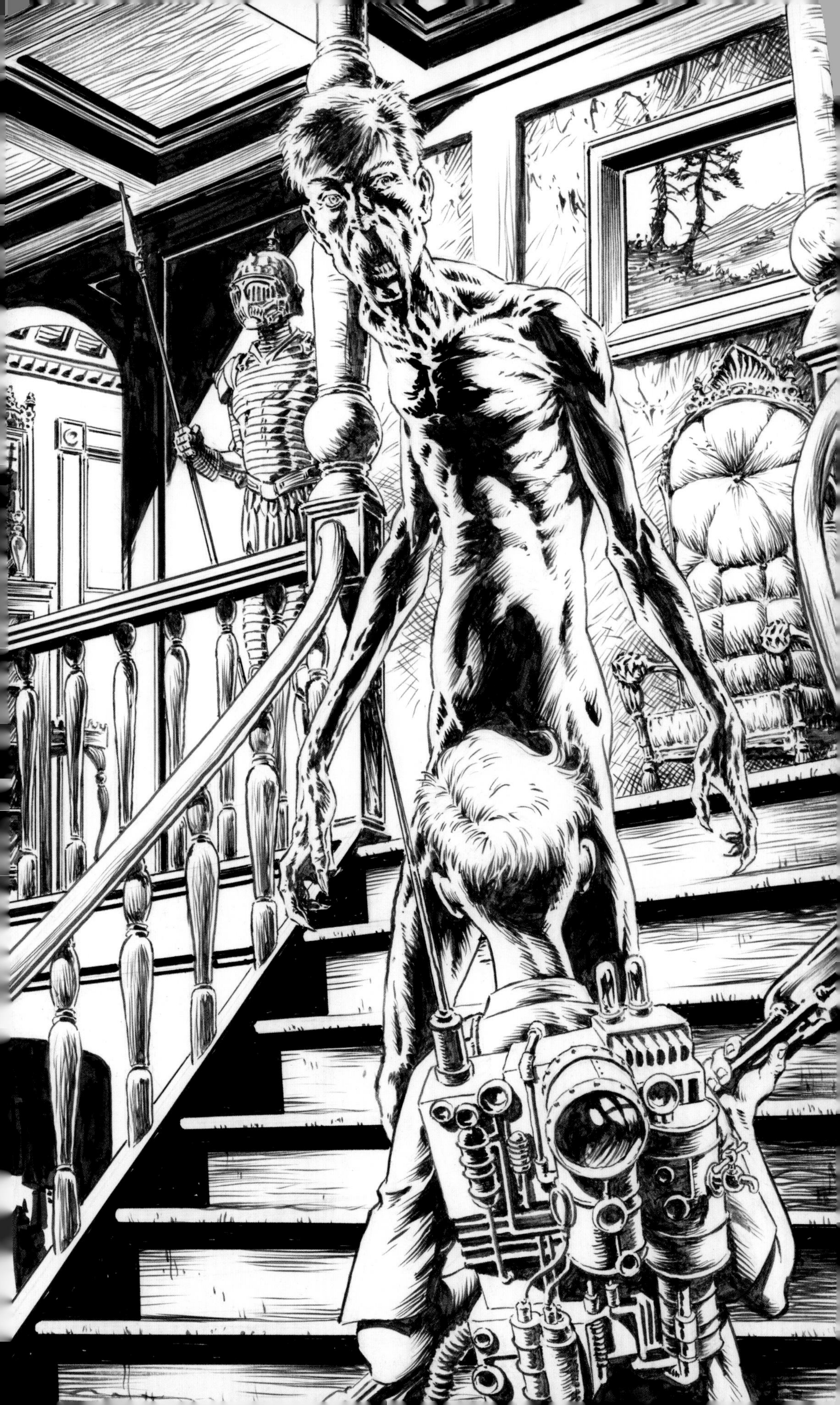

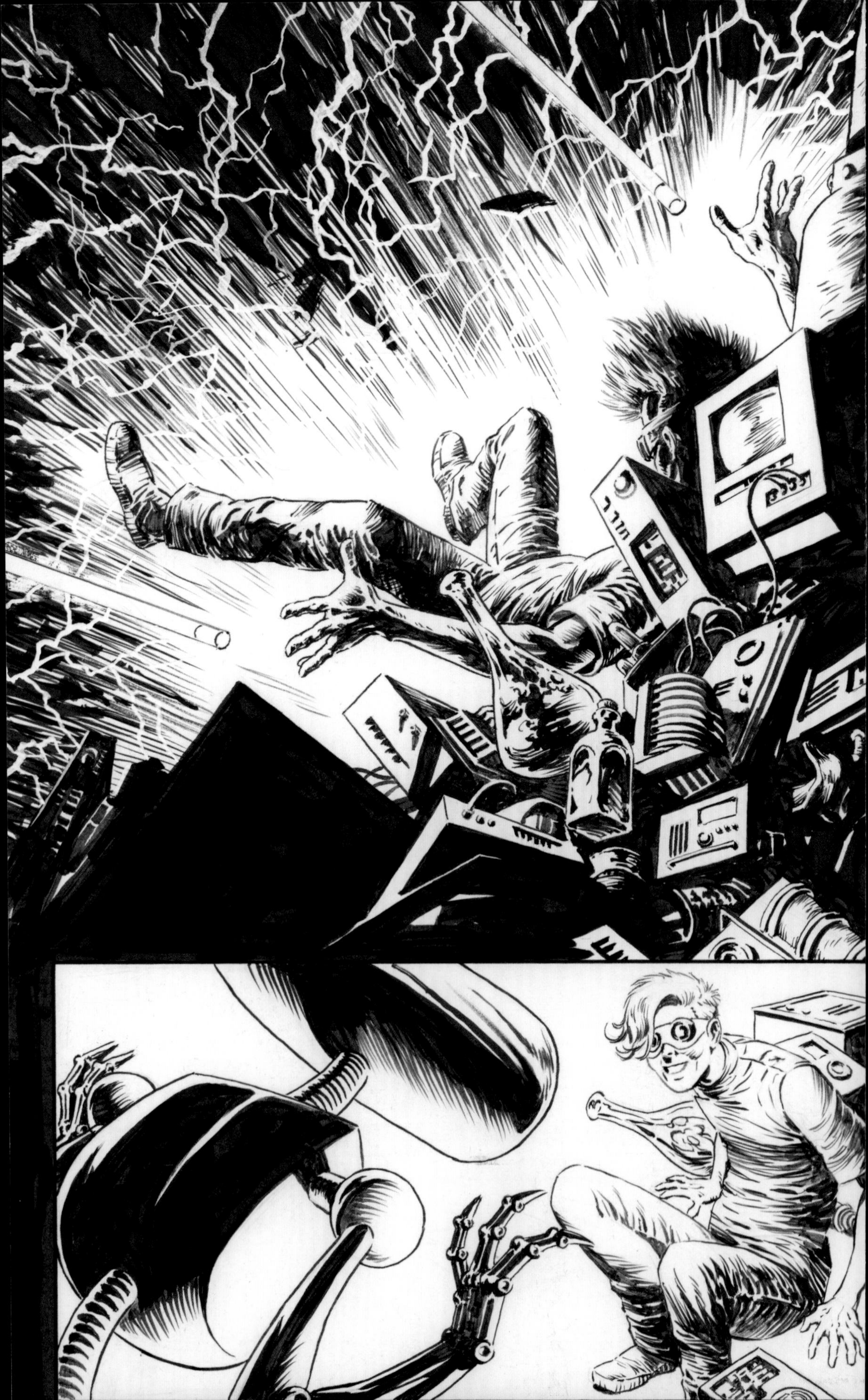

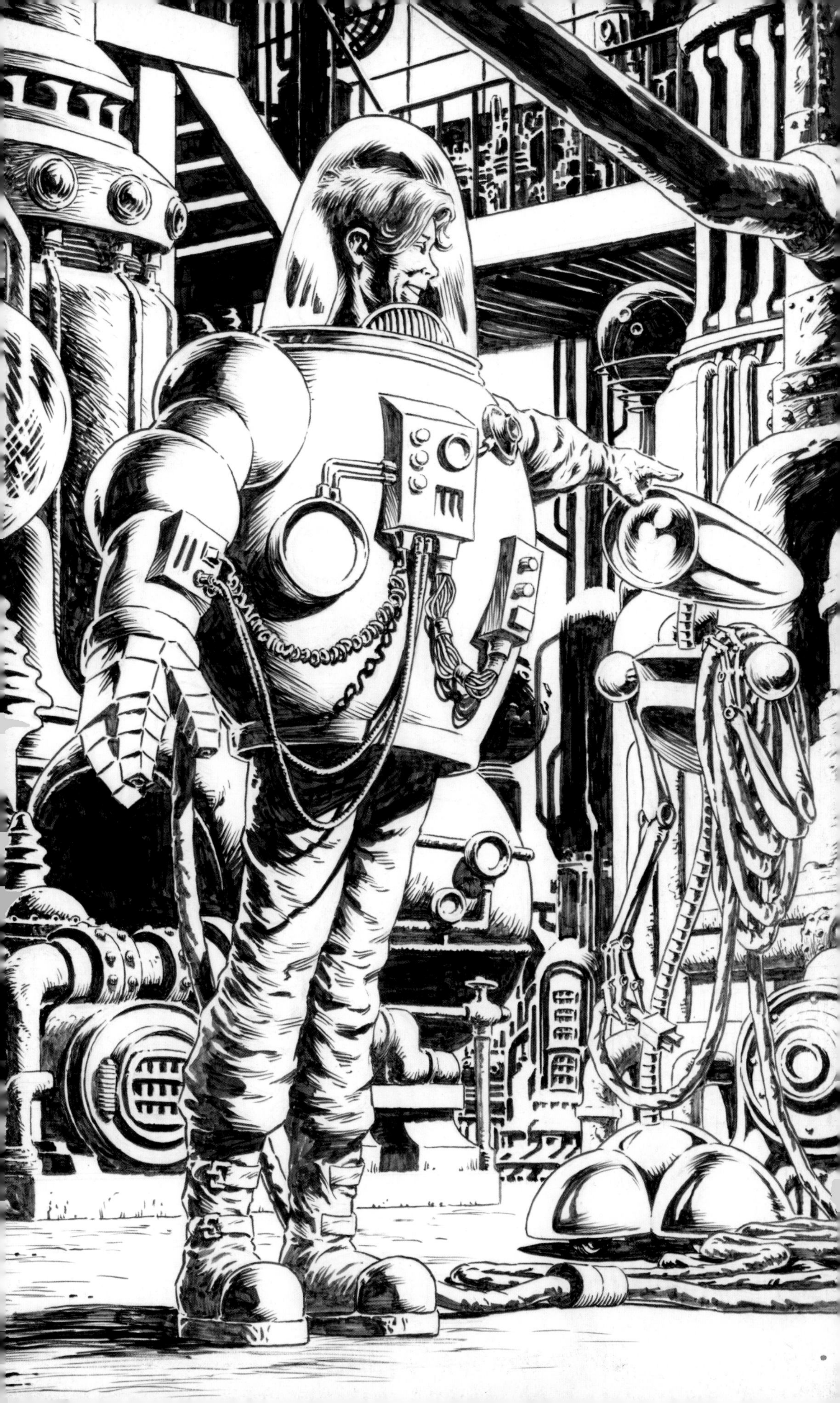

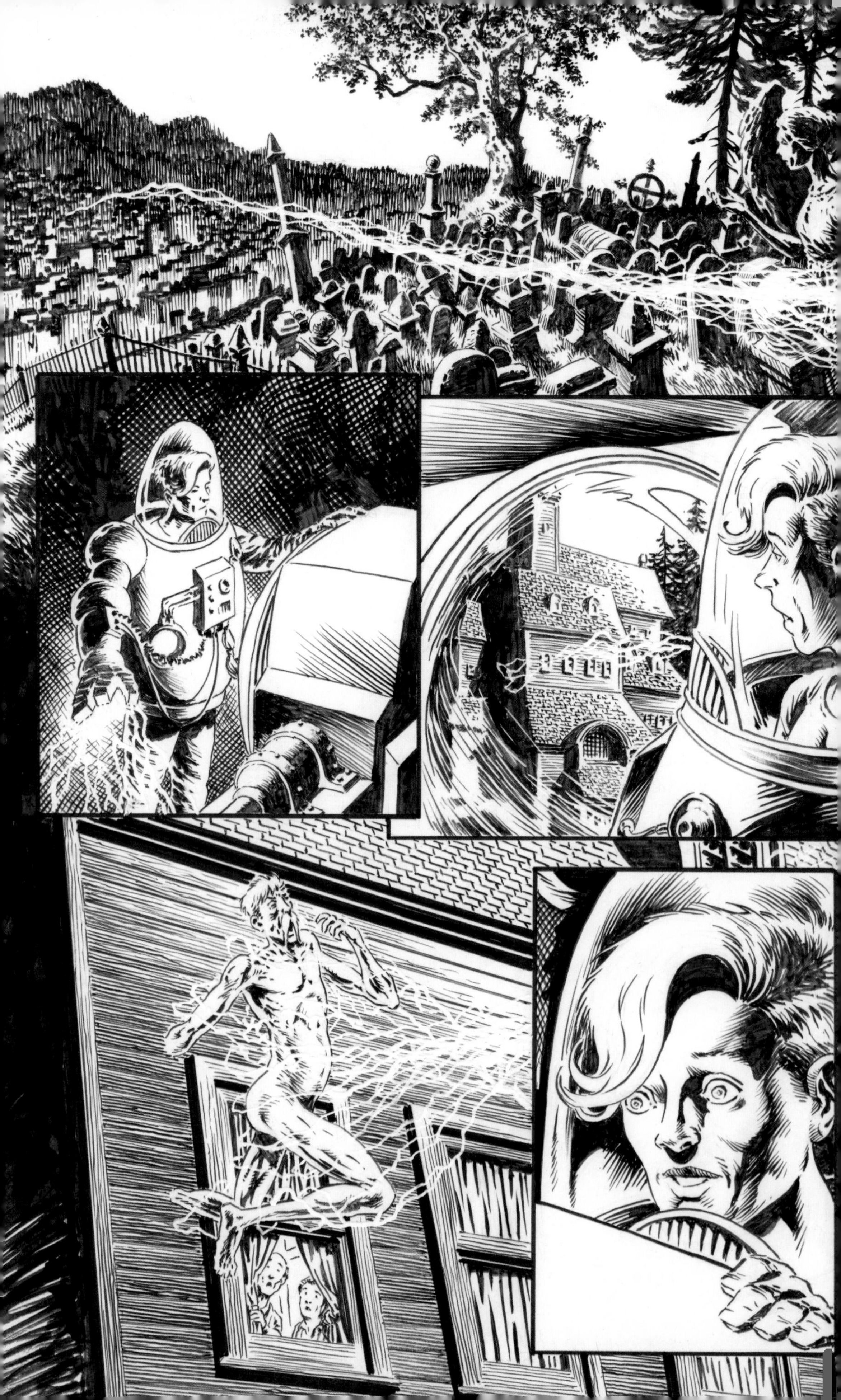

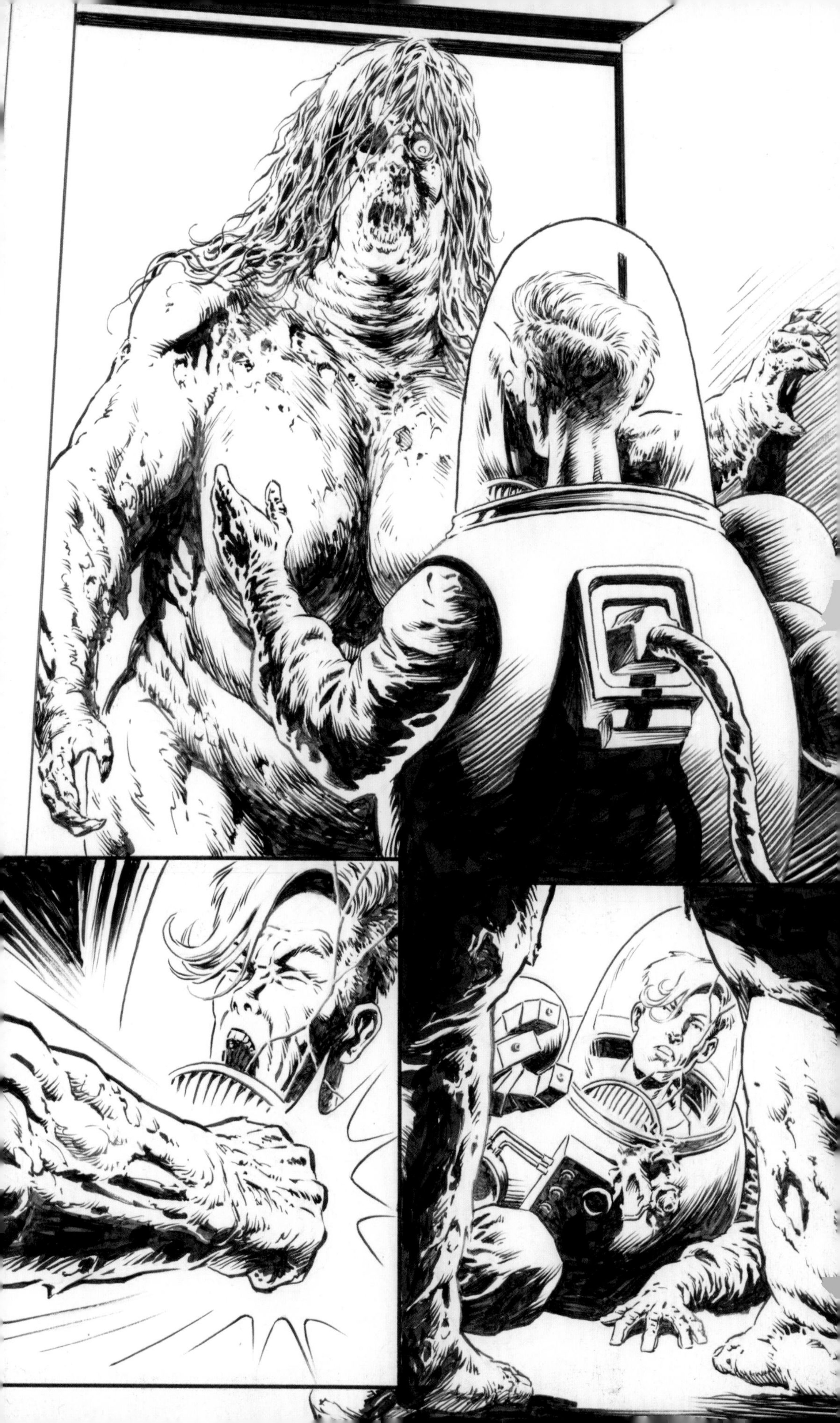

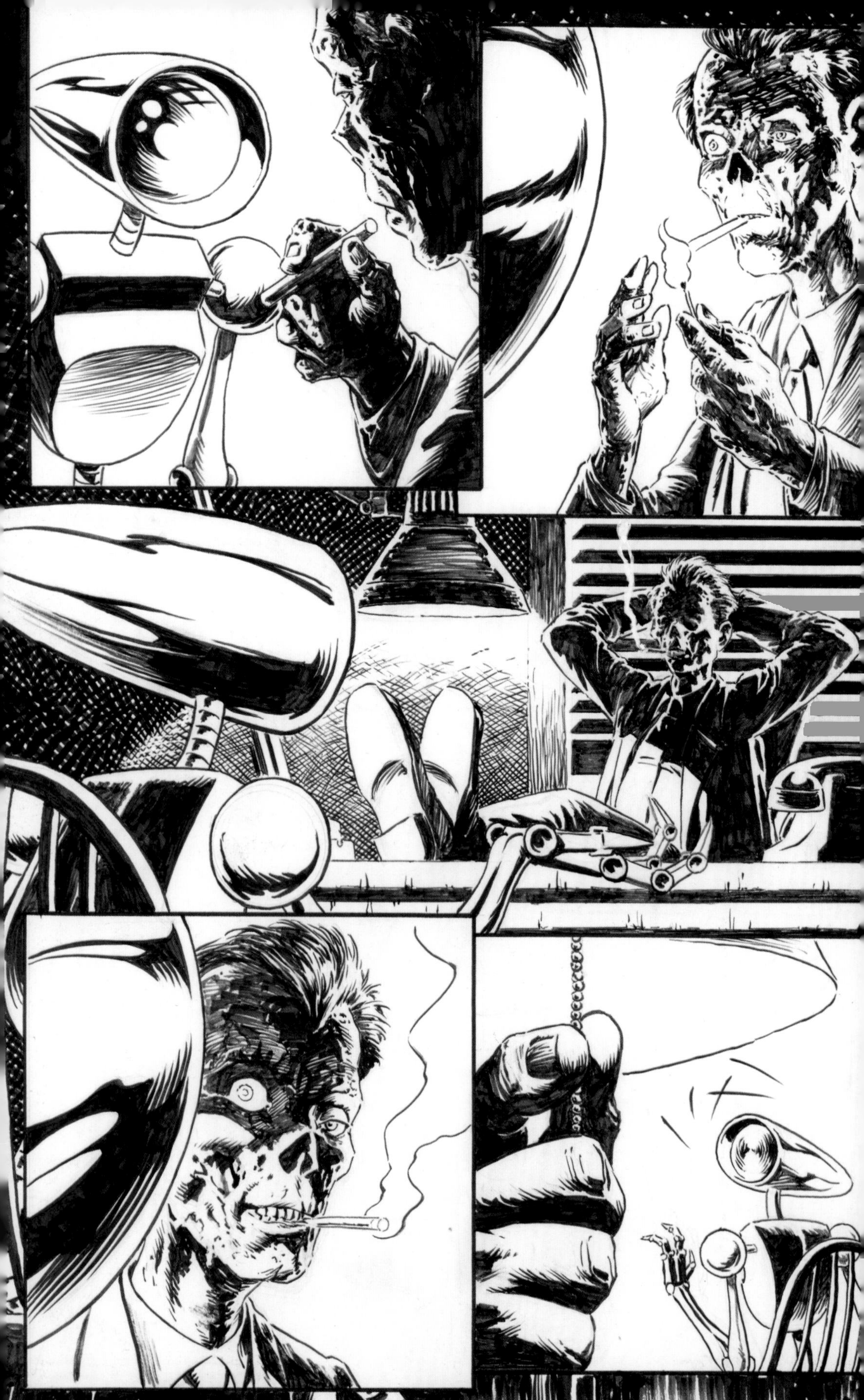

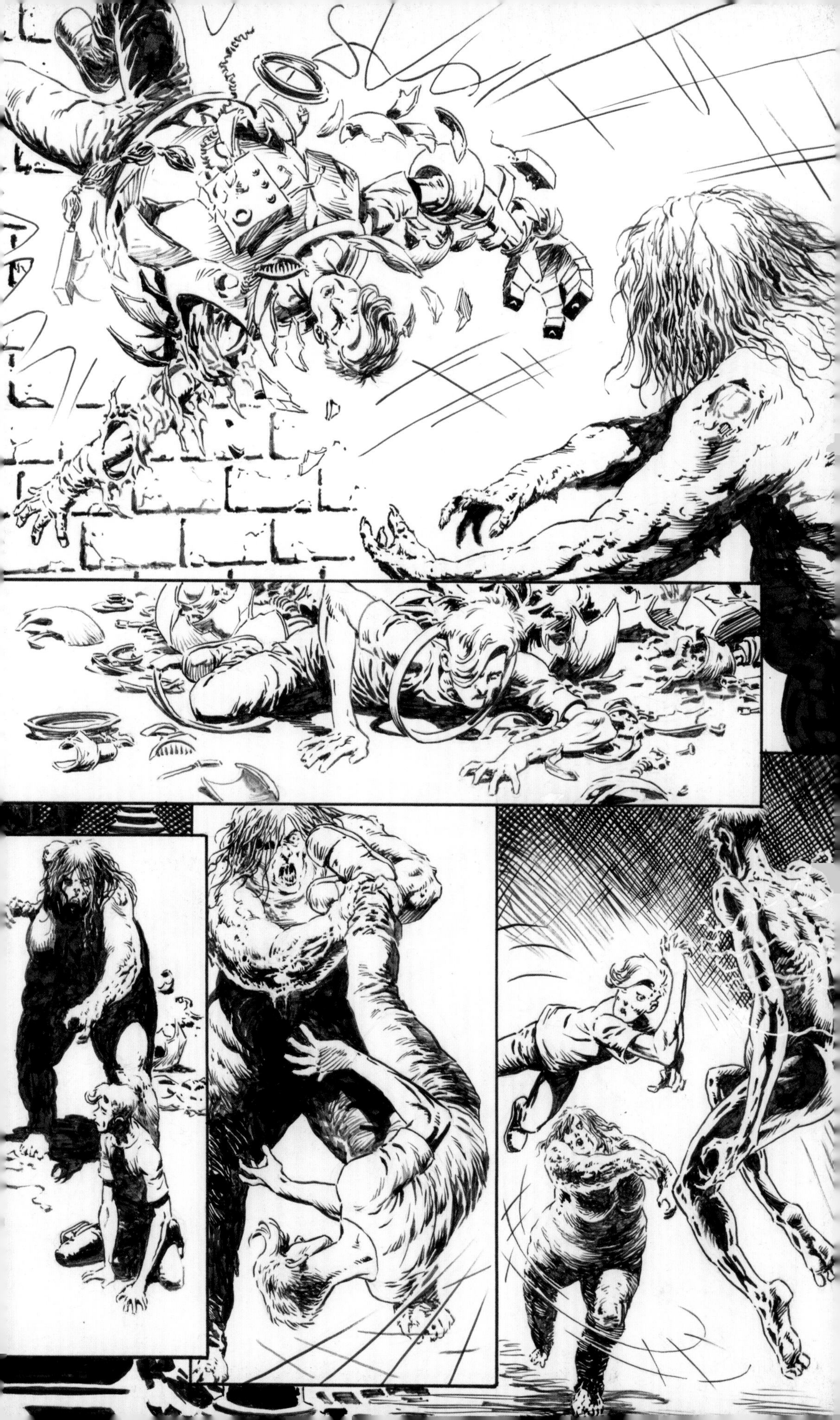

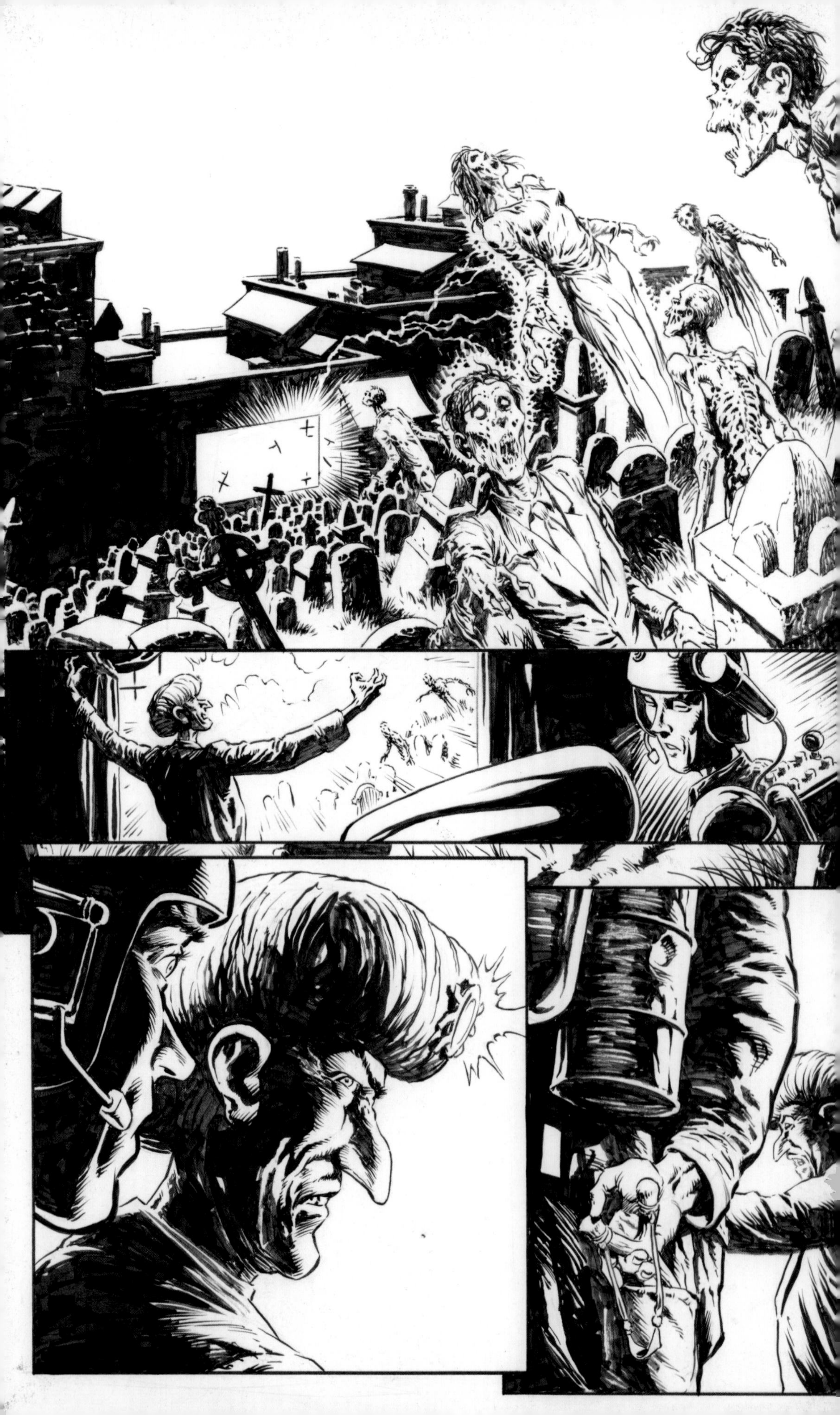

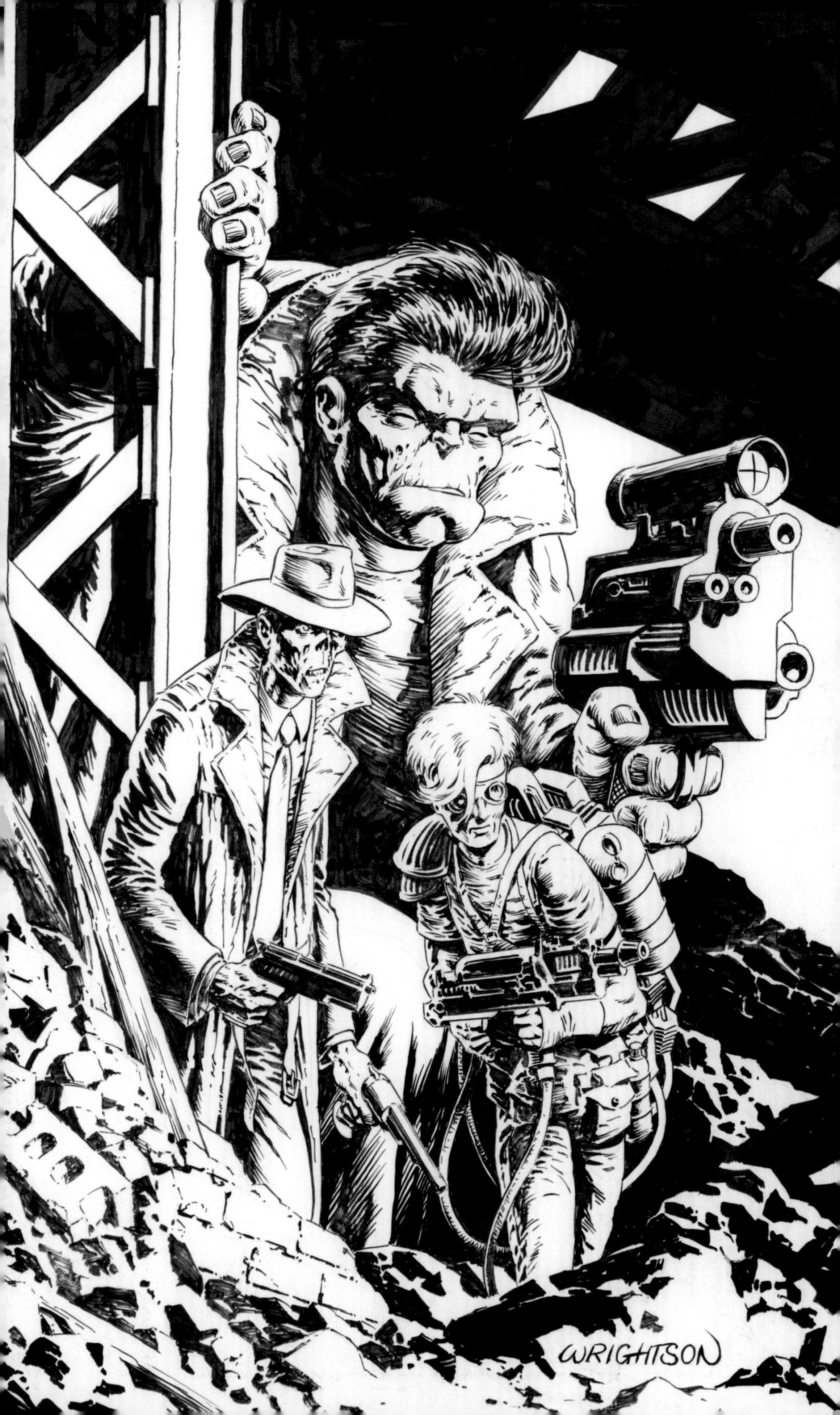
WRIGHTSON

STEVE NILES was named by FANGORIA magazine as one of its 13 rising talents who promise to keep us terrified for the next 25 years. His 30 DAYS OF NIGHT graphic novel sparked renewed interest in the horror genre. His other titles include SIMON DARK, BATMAN: GOTHAM AFTER MIDNIGHT, and CRIMINAL MACABRE. He recently completed MYSTERY SOCIETY and EDGE OF DOOM for IDW.

Bernie Wrightson

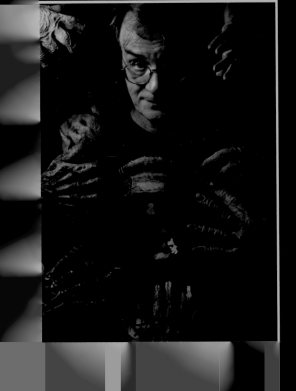

Legendary artist BERNIE WRIGHTSON has been creating horror art for over 40 years. Best known for co-creating (with writer Len Wein) the comic character SWAMP THING, and for definitively illustrating MARY SHELLEY'S FRANKENSTEIN, Bernie also collaborates regularly with author Stephen King, having illustrated THE STAND, CYCLE OF THE WEREWOLF, and the DARK TOWER V. He's worked on SPIDERMAN, BATMAN, and THE PUNISHER, and provided painted covers for the DC comics NEVERMORE and GEORGE ROMERO'S TOE TAGS. He wrote and drew his own sci-fi mini-series, CAPTAIN STERNN. Recent works include CITY OF OTHERS (Dark Horse Publishing) and DEAD SHE SAID and THE GHOUL (IDW Publishing) all co-created with popular author STEVE NILES. Today, Bernie resides in Los Angeles with his wife, Liz, where he works both on film designs and his own pet projects, including comic books, character designs for animation, and creepy drawings just for fun! Visit Bernie's